A

BIOGRAPHICAL SKETCH

OF

SIR HENRY HAVELOCK, K.C.B.

A

BIOGRAPHICAL SKETCH

OF

SIR HENRY HAVELOCK, K.C.B.

BY THE

REV. WILLIAM BROCK.

GYAN

Published by

GYAN

Gyan Publishing House
5, Ansari Road
Daryaganj, New Delhi-110002
Phone: 011-47034999, 9811692060
E-mail: books@gyanbooks.com

Distribution Network
gyanbooks.com
India, USA, Canada, UK, Australia

ISBN: 978-93-6208-102-5 (PB)
First Published, 1858

2nd Impression 2024

Printed at: Gyan Press, Delhi.

A BIOGRAPHICAL SKETCH OF SIR HENRY HAVELOCK, K.C.B.

Author: REV. WILLIAM BROCK

A BIOGRAPHICAL SKETCH

OF

SIR HENRY HAVELOCK, K.C.B.

A BIOGRAPHICAL SKETCH

OF

SIR HENRY HAVELOCK, K.C.B.

BY THE

REV. WILLIAM BROCK.

M.DCCC.LXIV.

TO

LADY HAVELOCK

WHO FOR EIGHT-AND-TWENTY YEARS

WAS THE LOVED COMPANION AND AFFECTIONATE WIFE

OF

A DEVOTED AND AFFECTIONATE HUSBAND,

This Sketch

OF

MAJOR-GENERAL SIR HENRY HAVELOCK, K.C.B.,

IS,

WITH HER LADYSHIP'S ESPECIAL PERMISSION,

RESPECTFULLY DEDICATED,

BY HER FAITHFUL SERVANT IN CHRIST,

WILLIAM BROCK.

PREFACE.

In deference to a very generally expressed desire for some authentic information about Sir Henry Havelock, the following biographical sketch, having special reference to his religious character, has been prepared: far too hastily, it must be confessed. The call, however, was too sudden and urgent to allow delay, and the book goes forth to the public with no merits but those which it derives from the trustworthiness of its statements and representations concerning one of the most illustrious men of the present age. By the General's family and friends their trustworthiness is avouched. To Lady Havelock the Editor's most grateful acknowledgments are due, for the kindness with which she has communicated so many of Sir Henry's letters, from which his countrymen and the world will learn authentically how good as well as how great a man he was whose loss they so unfeignedly deplore.

To Miss Havelock, and to other relatives of the General, who have rendered valuable aid to the Editor, thanks are cordially given for their effective co-operation.

Mr Marshman has assisted most generously, both by supplying valuable information, and by offering such counsel to the Editor as his acquaintance with the facts enabled him to supply.

By Sir William Norris permission was accorded in the kindest manner to use MS. drawn up at his request by Sir Henry Havelock, and which has been inserted in full under the title of "Fragmentary Memoranda."

In the preparation of the narrative of Havelock's most memorable "hundred days," from the date of his command to the relief of Lucknow, advantage has been taken of every available source of information; and though different representations may be expected of the same events, according to the point of view from which they were observed by the narrators, it is believed that in the following pages the reader will find an accurate account of the last campaign of the man who was so well designated by Lord Hardinge, "Every inch a soldier, and every inch a Christian."

A Memoir in full of this Christian soldier will

be published by his brother-in-law, Mr Marshman, as soon as the important documents in his possession can be duly examined and the results be prepared for the public eye.

The Biographer of Sir Henry Havelock will be Mr Marshman.

CONTENTS.

CHAPTER V.

HAVELOCK'S FRAGMENTARY MEMORANDA FROM 1827 TO 1849.

CHAPTER VI.

HAVELOCK'S VISIT TO ENGLAND.

CHAPTER VII.

HAVELOCK'S DOMESTIC SOLITUDE.

CHAPTER VIII.

HAVELOCK IN PERSIA.

CHAPTER IX.

HAVELOCK'S TIMELY RETURN TO INDIA.

CHAPTER X.

CAWNPORE AND LUCKNOW.

CHAPTER XI.

HAVELOCK'S ADVANCE TO CAWNPORE.

CHAPTER XII.

ENCOUNTERS WITH NANA SAHIB.

CHAPTER XIII.

HAVELOCK'S FIRST ADVANCE TO LUCKNOW.

CHAPTER XIV.

THE MARCH TO THE ALUM BAGH.

CHAPTER XV.

THE SIEGE OF THE RESIDENCY.

CHAPTER XVI.

THE RELIEF OF LUCKNOW.

CHAPTER XVII.

THE RESCUE ACCOMPLISHED.

CHAPTER XVIII.

HAVELOCK'S PEACEFUL DEATH.

CHAPTER XIX.

CONCLUSION.

CHAPTER I.

INTRODUCTION.

The Indian army has been rich in good men. Both among officers and private soldiers there has been a remarkable number of intelligent and earnest disciples of the Lord Jesus Christ. Many of them went to India Christian men: many of them have from time to time been converted there through the ministry of the chaplains and missionaries to whom they have been introduced.

No unusual thing is it to find amongst the foremost of our speakers at public meetings, amongst the members of our committees for benevolent objects, and amongst the hard-working practical philanthropists throughout the country, retired Indian officers, whose aim it is to serve their own generation according to the will of God.

Now and then, too, may be found amongst our aged and superannuated poor, some old soldier who, whilst loquacious about his exploits in siege and battle, is mindful of sermons which he heard from Thomason, and of prayer-meetings which were conducted by Chamberlain, and of things which were talked about concerning Buchanan, and Brown, and Carey, and Marshman, and Ward, and Henry Martyn. He delights to tell how a Christian church was formed in his regiment, and how comrade after comrade was induced to believe in Christ, and how brethren from other regiments occasionally joined their worship, and how on more than one occasion God called a man so evidently to the preaching of the gospel, that his discharge was obtained, that he might give himself continually to prayer and the ministry of the word. And that which the conduct of our retired East Indian officers, and the conversations of our superannuated East Indian soldiers, indicate, our earlier missionary annals directly confirm. When depressed by the apparent failure of their efforts to instruct the heathen, the missionaries were frequently encouraged by their success amongst their own countrymen in the army; and they were also often cheered by the arrival in their neighbourhood of some fellow-helpers to the truth, either amongst the officers or the men.

And this peculiarity, with some vicissitudes, has continued to the present time, when such men as the Lawrences, Nicholson, Edwardes, Montgomery, Havelock, and many others, have proved themselves so indubitably good soldiers of Jesus Christ. Trustworthy evidence warrants the assertion that a goodly number of the younger men in India are following steadily in the footsteps of these illustrious ones; so steadily, indeed, that no intimations of displeasure from the authorities at home will prevent their hearty personal co-operation for the promulgation of the gospel.

The Christian people of England may rest assured that their protest against any further compromise of evangelical truth in India will be effectively sustained, and that their demand for most unqualified permission to preach and teach Christ there will be followed up in India itself; and by none more resolutely than by the men to whom, to a large extent, the management of our military affairs will successively be consigned. They will not consent to withdraw their names from the subscription lists of Bible and Missionary associations. They will not be parties to the pantheistic practice of serving God one day and Belial the next. They will not sanction the opinion that as Christianity is good for one man, so idolatry is good for another man. Their ground is taken, and will certainly be maintained, that whilst the natives must not be forced to profess Christianity, there shall be no obstacle thrown in their way by the Government, if they desire to acknowledge themselves disciples of Christ. At least, they will lend neither conntenance nor help to the continuance of that Indian traditionary policy, at the fuller disclosure and justification of which the British public has recently been so much surprised.

This is cause for sincere congratulation, seeing what will be the probable difficulties attendant on the changes which must now be made. Should they be all we can desire, then good men will be needed to carry them into effect, or they will practically be defeated. Should they be found unsuitable or inadequate, then good men will be needed for the prevention of mischief and the correction of mistakes. Our Indian army promises to provide such men. And for them may be claimed the grateful respect of all their brethren in the faith. No child's play is the work which will devolve upon them. No walking in silver slippers, as Bunyan puts it, will be the maintenance of their allegiance to Christ. Their obligation to decide, at an emergency, how best to act will be found no easy task.

A recent instance may serve to shew this. An officer who had been appointed by Sir John Lawrence as the Resident in Cashmere, found himself soon and suddenly called upon to pronounce on a case of threatened suttee. The population of the place was in a state of great excitement against the English, and the solitary representative of the Government was in a position of imminent jeopardy. He was already well-nigh at his wits' end, when, to complete his embarrassment, the Rajah, who had been friendly, died. Nothing seemed impending now but death for the officer and his wife and children. To their dismay, they learned that several of the wives of the deceased determined that they would burn on his funeral pile. This, however, they could not lawfully do without the express permission of this solitary Englishman. It was formally applied for. What should he do ? He had no soldiery to fall back upon. He had no retreat from the violence of the people, who were already much exasperated. He knew the priests were urging on the masses to demand the requisite permission, while the women were actually arrayed in bridal dresses for what they believed would be a celestial marriage. Lying on his bed, for he was a great sufferer at the time, he determined in God's strength that he would refuse the permission. At any risk to himself or his family, he would not lend himself to an act of which he intensely disapproved. He sought for wisdom, and it was given to him liberally. Calling the official to him who was awaiting his decision, he reminded him of a passage in the sacred books of the Seiks which spoke of something that was better for the widow than the actual suttee. Then he told him of the well-known discouragement which had been given by the deceased prince for many years to the practice of suttee. Then he assured him that the English nation, whose friendship it was his interest to cultivate, would be grieved and offended should the suttee take place. He urged these several considerations to the utmost of his power, and concluded his remonstrance by an earnest entreaty that the intention should be given up, expressly refusing at any rate the permission for which they sought. He then bravely abided the result.

To his inexpressible satisfaction it was resolved to

relinquish the ceremony for which the preparations had been made, and without any outbreak or mischief it actually was abandoned.

For such Christian firmness, in connexion with such Christian prudence, it becometh us to be sincerely thankful; and, knowing that men of this character are to be found all through our Indian army, there is reason why we should be devoutly glad. They deserve our esteem; they have a claim upon our prayers. The claim, too, comes, with equal force upon all their Christian countrymen, whether they believe or disbelieve in the justifiableness of war. Without any unfaithfulness to their general principle, those who hold that war and Christianity are irreconcilable may regard such men as Lawrence and Colonel Gardiner with sincere respect. Whilst abiding by their own convictions, they may remember that those God-fearing men in our army are acting conscientiously; and thus, though their profession may be deplored and deprecated, their characters may be admired. The occasion is an auspicious one for evincing our admiration of them. They will appreciate it warmly amidst their manifold temptations, and greatly will they be encouraged by the assurances of our sympathy and prayer to God on their behalf. Under God, more than we can imagine depends upon them, and will depend on them, in the transition which India is preparing to undergo. Their indirect influence will be incalculable. The influence they will exert immediately will be quite as great. In friendly and Christian intercourse with the enlightened civil servants of the Crown, they will be successful hindrances to the perpetration of evil, and valuable helps to the accomplishment of good. Of the patronage of idolatry they will be ashamed, and against official attendance on its services they will protest. The European community in India, wrought upon by their example, will give up evil habits, whilst the native communities will be made to feel that the Christian religion is a reality, and not a sham; a religion, too, which, for its practical benignity and power, deserves to be examined by them, and personally received. By moral influence, rather than by the use of the sword, our devout soldiers will facilitate the ultimate results which we are anticipating from the terrible revolt—even the coming of that kingdom which is righteousness, and joy, and peace in the Holy Ghost. That the mutineers thought evil against us there can be no doubt. God, however, will overrule their machinations for the accomplishment of good; and Havelock's wishes and prayers will be answered, that India might be freed from abominable idolatries, and her sons and daughters become emancipated with the glorious liberty of the children of God.

CHAPTER II.

HAVELOCK'S TRAINING AND DESTINATION.

WHETHER the attempt to trace out an illustrious Danish lineage for Havelock has been successful may be left undecided. He says nothing on the subject in his papers, contenting himself with a simple statement of the birthplace of his parents, and of their English descent. Enough for him that he came of a virtuous stock, and that he was trained up in the nurture and admonition of the Lord.

The following is his own account:—

"Born at Bishop Wearmouth, near Sunderland, in the county of Durham, 5th April 1795, which happened to be Lady-day, old style, and Easter-Sunday, new style.

"Earliest recollections are to be dated 1798, when parents and family were residing at Ford, near Sunderland.

"My father, who had been engaged in commerce and ship-building at Sunderland, migrated to the south of England in September 1799.

"He purchased Ingress, near Dartford, in the county of Kent, October 1799.

"My father, William Havelock, descended from a family which formerly resided at Grimsby in Lincolnshire, and was himself born at Guisborough, in Yorkshire. After his first improvement of fortune at Sunderland he married Jane, daughter of John Carter, a conveyancer of Stockton-on-Tees, whose wife was the sister of William Ettrick, Esq., of High Barnes, near Sunderland, a man of ancient family, and landed property in the county of Durham, which had belonged to it for many generations.

"At the time of our settlement in Kent my brothers and sisters were—

"1. Helen, born 1792; died in 1825, or thereabout.

"2. William, born 1793, January 23d, fell in the cavalry action at Ramnugger, in the Punjaub, November 22d, 1843.

"3. Jane, born 1798; married to an officer of the Royal Navy; still living.

"There were born afterwards, at Ingress—

"4. Thomas, born in 1800; died of fever at Vittoria, in Spain, with Sir De Lacy Evans's army.

"5. Isabella, born 1802; married to John Moore Cave, Esq., of one of the Bristol families of that name; died at Leghorn, whilst travelling towards Florence, in 1825.

"6. Charles Frederick, born 1803; still living, a Major in the army, and served with distinction in

India, chiefly with the cavalry." (Now Major-General Havelock, late of the Turkish Contingent.)

"In January 1801, William and Henry went to school at Dartford, as parlour-boarders, with the Rev. J. Bradley, the Curate of Swanscomb, in which parish Ingress was situated."

We have here, in Havelock's own words, the simple narrative of his parentage and brotherhood; written, it will be observed, not in the first person, but in the third, when he is speaking of himself. This peculiarity he maintained throughout his paper.

He remained with Mr Bradley until 1804, disporting himself, in the intervals of school-work, without much restraint, either out of doors or in, at Ingress Park.

Cool judgment, calculation, and forethought were frequently evinced, along with an amount of fearlessness at which his father was surprised. "Were you not frightened," said he once to him, "when you fell off that tree just now?" "No; I had too much else to do to be frightened. I was thinking about the bird's eggs." And away he walked.

He was a great reader of all papers on which he could lay his hands relating to military affairs. With the movements of Napoleon he made himself familiar, and evinced such tendencies towards the profession of a soldier that his mother apprehended the disappointment of her project of educating him for the law.

It was observed by his master one day that Havelock had a black eye, and he was required to say what had been going on. "It came there," was the boy's only answer. "How did it come?" He was imperturbably silent, and a sound thrashing was the result. The fact was, that he had been interfering for a schoolfellow who was not getting fair play in a fight, and in his zeal for his friend had got disfigured. Not that he was at all a pugnacious boy at home or at school. He was a boy every inch of him, there was no doubt, and knew very well how to hold his own against all comers. But he was remarkable rather for quietness than noisiness—a steady-going, reflective, self-contained kind of boy. "Old Phlos" was the familiar *sobriquet* by which he was known by his companions—a corruption, at least a contraction, it is presumed, of the ambiguous word philosopher,—just such a contraction, dashed with a little humour, as might have well been looked for had the future character of the different boys been known. It indicated that incipient discernment on the part of Havelock's companions for which afterwards many of them were remarkable. It described Havelock himself exactly. His subsequent devisings and doings in scenes of extremest danger proved him to be a philosopher above many of his associates—a thoroughly wise man.

His own narrative may be resumed :—

"1804.—October, Removed to the Charterhouse,

and located in the boarding-house of the Rev. Dr Matthew Raine, then Head Master.

"My most intimate friends at the Charterhouse were Samuel Hinds, William Norris, and Julius Charles Hare. Hinds, a man of taste and a poet, spent his early years in travelling, married in France, distinguished himself in one of the colonial assemblies of his native island, Barbadoes, at the period of slave emancipation, and died at Bath about 1847.

"Norris, now Sir William Norris, was called to the bar, appointed successively Advocate Fiscal, or Queen's Advocate, Puisne Judge, and Chief Justice at Ceylon, and subsequently Recorder of Penang.

"Hare went to Trinity College, Cambridge, in 1812, graduated B.A. 1815, and subsequently as M.A., became a Fellow and Tutor at Trinity. He is well known to the literary and religious world by his joint translation with Dr Connop Thirlwall of part of the Roman History of Niebuhr, some volumes of sermons, and several polemical pamphlets.

"Nearly cotemporary with me and the boys just named were Connop Thirlwall, now Bishop of St David's; George Waddington, Dean of Durham, distinguished as a scholar and a man of letters; George Grote, the historian of Greece; Archdeacon Hale, now Master of the Charterhouse; Alderman Thompson, the member for Westmoreland; Sir William MacNaghten, the talented but unfortunate Envoy to Cabool; the Right Honourable Fox Maule, now Secretary at War; Eastlake, the painter; and Yates, the actor."

"In April 1810, Henry Havelock had gone up into that fifth form, of which Walpole, grandson of Sir Robert, was first, Hare second, John Pindar third, and Havelock fourth. It consisted of some thirty boys, and lower down in it were Connop Thirlwall and Hinds."

"In 1811, Havelock passed in due course into the sixth form. Dr Raine, the learned and accomplished Head Master, died in August, and was succeeded by Dr Russell; and in December of the same year Havelock left the Charterhouse."

He looked back to his time spent there with the greatest satisfaction, especially on account of the grounding that he obtained in the Latin and Greek classics. His initiation into an acquaintance with the great models of antiquity was most effective: and to his familiarity with them he was indebted, as Mr Marshman testifies, for "the perspicuity, vigour, and purity of his own style."

Not merely thoughtful was the young Carthusian as a school-boy—he was religiously if not evangelically thoughtful. In his memoranda he says, "The most important part of the history of any man is his connexion through faith with the invisible world. So of Henry Havelock it may be recorded, that there were early indications of the strivings of the good Spirit of God in his soul, though Satan and the world were permitted for many years to triumph." Certainly whilst he was at the Charterhouse the evidence of those strivings was apparent; neither were they in vain. As early in his life as that, he knew what liabilities to scorn and ridicule for conscience' sake were. "Methodist" was one current taunt; "canting hypocrite" was another, for any youngster who would dare to acknowledge God. However, he with several others, as eminent in their several professions afterwards as he was in his, outbraved the taunt. Without being ostentatious, they were faithful to their convictions, and regularly met in one of the sleeping-rooms of the Charterhouse for religious purposes. Sermons were read by them with one another, and conversations ensued upon the reading, as to the bearing of the truth on their own character and conduct.

How would any record of those juvenile exercises of devotion be prized now! To quote what Hare objected to Havelock's remarks—and what Hinds replied to Hare's objection—and what Norris advanced in support of the reply—and what John Pindar produced to shew that they were probably all wrong together—would both gratify a laudable curiosity and enable us to trace ultimate excellencies back to their earliest germs. Nothing, however, was recorded, and we must be content with the results. "Old Phlos" became more and more grounded and settled in his resolution to fear God. The lovers of pleasure might seem to have the best of it. He did not pretend to any sort of stoicism whatever. He did not deny for a moment that what they said about fun and frolic was true. Old heads were not to be looked for on young shoulders. The doleful and the dismal would come fast enough without being fetched.

But then in his esteem the fear of God was neither doleful nor dismal in the least degree. He could cultivate that, and read Greek and Latin with any of them. He could search the Scriptures and pray to God, and yet do anything that it was manly or virtuous to do, either in the playground or elsewhere. There was nothing, indeed, either manly or virtuous that he was not all the more ready to do because in simplicity and godly sincerity he walked with God. His religion was a good deal more of a guardian angel than a ghost. His Christianity increased rather than diminished his enjoyment. His godliness felt that it had the promise of the life that now is, as well as of that which is to come.

As with so many others, the religious impressions of Havelock were traceable to the influence and the efforts of his mother when he was a little boy. It was her custom to assemble her children for reading the Scriptures and prayer in her own room. Henry was always of the party whenever he was at home, and in course of time he was expected to take the reading, which he generally did. Under these pleasant circumstances he knew, like Timothy, the Holy Scriptures from a child.

After the death of his mother his religious feelings fluctuated considerably, and at length he became dissatisfied with the generally-received opinions of the character and the work of Christ. It was necessary for him, the doubt having been once originated and entertained, to go thoroughly into that question. He listened to the arguments which were addressed to him against the divinity and the atonement of the Saviour, and at one time he thought that they were conclusive. He might almost have been claimed as a believer in the Unitarian creed.

Subsequent investigations, however, convinced him that he had been committing some great mistakes. He had been forgetting that his business was not with that which was antecedently probable about Christ, but with that which was actually written about Him in the Old and New Testaments. He had been overlooking the obligation to take the entire testimony of Scripture, and to accept everything which, when honestly interpreted, it is found to teach. Because he was unable to understand how Jesus Christ could be both human and divine, he had pronounced that He could not be so—that the idea of such union was impossible and absurd. But no sooner did he recognise the authoritative nature of the Divine oracles, and the corresponding duty of receiving their communications on the subject without objection, than he renounced all his disbelief and doubt, and held fast to the doctrine,—That whilst the Saviour is the man Christ Jesus, He is at the same time over all, God blessed for evermore.

The time having come for devoting himself to some profession, the decision was given for the law, in accordance with the well-known wishes of his mother. Not enthusiastic was he; but he was well content to work at Coke upon Littleton, and if necessary, to encounter the statutes at large. Accordingly, in 1814, he became a pupil of Chitty's, "the great special pleader of the day," as he described him, and addressed himself to the task of preparing to be a lawyer. Talfourd was a fellow-clerk with him, and they became sincere and attached friends. Mr Marshman tells how he has heard Havelock refer to this acquaintance with Talfourd. "A congeniality of habits brought them into close intimacy, and when they left the chambers of Chitty, they beguiled many an hour in walking up and down over their favourite resort, Westminster Bridge; but their conversation was of other matters than the pleas of the Crown, and turned much oftener on the beauties of poetry than upon the contents of musty parchments. Havelock used to observe, in after life, that the last time they took their stroll on the bridge, when he was about to embrace the military profession, Talfourd noticed the placid progress of the stream under the arches, and repeated with ecstasy that line of Wordsworth—

'The river glideth at its own sweet will.'"

Not to be overlooked is the memorable death of

these two great men so many years afterwards; the one on the bench, at Stafford, whilst right eloquently pleading for greater sympathy between rich and poor; the other in the camp at Lucknow, exhausted by his exertions for relieving helpless women and children from disgrace and death.

With the law, however, Havelock was not destined to become familiar. In the year in which his mother died, (1810,) his brother William entered the army, commencing his active career at the battle of the Coa. This circumstance drew Henry's attention again towards military pursuits; and when Napoleon returned from Elba, in 1815, "he yielded," as he says, "to the military propensities of his race," by asking his brother to get him a commission forthwith.

There was some delay, but having greatly distinguished himself at Waterloo, as aide-de-camp to Baron Altern, his brother—"oné of the most chivalrous officers of the British service"—became a more influential man, and he at once exerted himself on Henry's behalf. About a month after the battle of Waterloo, "Henry was appointed second lieutenant in the Rifle Brigade, then the 95th."

Under these circumstances Havelock's destination in life was changed and definitively fixed. He saw an opportunity for making his way honourably, of which, through the reverses in his family fortunes, he felt bound to take advantage; and having no scruples about the compatibility of war with Christianity, he became a soldier. He exchanged the pen for the sword. Instead of giving himself to read Blackstone, he took up Vauban for careful study. Where he would have had to devote attention to "cases," he came to write "despatches." For a Generalship rather than for a Judgeship, was he henceforward a competitor. His fellow-student at special pleading rose to be Mr Justice Talfourd, of the Common Pleas. He rose to be gazetted as Sir Henry Havelock, of Lucknow.

"Having thus entered the army," says Mr Marshman, "he gave his whole soul up to his profession. He read every military memoir and history within his reach. He laid in a rich store of information for his future guidance. He became familiar with every memorable battle and siege of ancient or modern times, and examined the detail and the result of every movement in the field with the eye of a soldier. Frequently has he delighted his friends in India by fighting over again the actions of Blenheim and Austerlitz, and the other memorable battles of Marlborough and Napoleon, calling up from memory the strength and disposition of each division of the contending forces, and tracing on paper their successive movements till he came to the critical movement which, in his opinion, decided the fate of the day. His great aim was to master the principles of the art of war, which he always affirmed to be unalterable, and which no General could neglect without risk of failure. The history of our own military achievements became perfectly familiar to him, and he could refer from memory to the services of every British regiment in the Army List. For several years he continued to serve in England, Scotland, and Ireland, constantly adding to his stock of observation and knowledge. In 1821, he travelled through France and Italy, and never failed to visit and examine the fields on which great actions had been fought."

CHAPTER III.

HAVELOCK'S VOYAGE AND ARRIVAL IN INDIA.

No very active service awaited the subaltern for some time. "He served," he writes, "in England, Ireland, and Scotland, in the interval between his first nomination and the year 1823, travelled in France and the north of Italy, read a good deal in a discursive way, and acquired some knowledge of his profession which was useful to him in after days." It was his lot again to fall in with men of mark, whose names were to become afterwards illustrious and renowned.

"He was subaltern in the 95th Rifle Brigade, and the present Sir Harry Smith, the victor of Aliwal, was his captain.

"Some time elapsed, and he was at length induced to look for an exchange. The augmentation of the 13th Light Infantry taking place, he was transposed to that regiment. He embarked for India in January 1823. It was his own choice to serve in this part of the world, and he had fitted himself for Indian service by studying Hindostanee and Persian under Dr Gilchrist, in London, before he left."

On his voyage an event occurred in relation to "the most important part of the history of a man's life," which he attributed most gratefully to the providence of a gracious God. For years he had known what it was to be anxious about his soul, and also about the performance of the Divine will. He felt that life had not been given to him to be spent exactly as he pleased. The Scriptures had not been put into his possession to be set at naught or disregarded. The Son of God had not died for him in sacrifice for sin, without having the strongest claim upon him for the most grateful and responsive love. All this had been at work upon him for years, with more or less activity and power; and it was at work upon him when he set sail for India. His condition appears to have been that of feeling after God, if haply he might find Him.

Somewhat like his military predecessor, mentioned in the tenth chapter of the Acts of the Apostles, the centurion of the Italian band at Cæsarea, Havelock was a devout man, and one that prayed to God alway; but he needed more instruction about the perfect freeness of salvation, or, at least, a clearer conception of his own welcome to the immediate participation of the good that Christ had lived and died to procure. He needed, in fact, very much what Cornelius needed; and in His sovereignty God supplied the need. The set time to favour the devout inquirer came. He has given his own account of the Divine interposition on his behalf:—

"A far more important event, as regarded the interests of the writer, ought to have been recorded whilst narrating the events of 1823; for it was while he was sailing across the wide Atlantic towards Bengal, that the Spirit of God came to him with its offers of peace and mandate of love, which, though for some time resisted, were received, and at length prevailed. There was wrought that great change in his soul which has been productive of unspeakable advantage to him in time, and he trusts has secured him happiness through eternity. The 'General Kyd,' in which he was embarked, conveyed to India Major Sale, destined thereafter to defend Jellalabad: but she also carried out a humble, unpretending man,—James Gardner, then a lieutenant in the 13th, now a retired captain, engaged in Home Missionary objects and other works of Christian benevolence at Bath. This excellent person was most influential in leading Havelock to make public avowal, by his works, of Christianity in earnest."

About this avowal there could be subsequently no mistake. He had found peace with God through Jesus Christ by the simple exercise of faith, accepting the offer which had been made to him of a present salvation, and obeying the mandate which had been pressed upon him there and then to believe. Accustomed as he was to the exercise of his intellectual faculties, and somewhat competent by his educational training to investigate and decide upon the merits of a case, he examined the claims of the so-called glad tidings upon his attention, and he decided that they were by all means to be received. It was not fanatical he felt convinced, but it was philosophical to accept the mission of Jesus Christ as Divine. It was not rash and inconclusive, but sound and justifiable to submit to the righteousness of God. He was the wise man who took the witness which had been given from heaven about forgiveness and remission of sins with reverence and godly fear; whilst he who acknowledged the authority of the New Testament, but gave no sort of heed to that witness, was not a wise man, but a fool. This Havelock always insisted upon. He maintained that so far from degrading his intellectual nature when he became a follower of Christ, he was bringing it into the loftiest employment to which it could be called. He was not deteriorating his moral nature when he sought to have fellowship with the sufferings of Christ, but was thereby securing its indefinite improvement, even its immediate and everlasting approximation to the perfection of the Most High God. Thus sanctifying the Lord God in his heart, he was ready always to give an answer to every man that asked him a reason of the hope that was in him with meekness and fear.

To those, indeed, who were willing to converse on the subject, he shewed that never were men more mistaken if they imagined that they must sacrifice their mental manhood in order to have faith in the Redeemer, or if they supposed that they must cease to employ their minds the moment they exercised faith in the Son of God. No pains did the Lord's freeman spare in the attempt to convince them that the exercise of faith in well-attested evidence is one of the noblest occupations of the mind, and that the employment of mental manhood in conforming oneself to Christ is the sublimest employment to which it can possibly attain.

Better, perhaps, than all his arguments to this effect, was his living example day by day. If a conversation was going on about any matter, literary, or scientific, or political, or artistic, Havelock could and did take his own part with the different groups, as much interested as any of them, and, with a few exceptions only, a good deal better read. His religious habits had quickened, and not petrified his powers. By his devoutness his tastes had been purified, and not debased. Godliness had not made him either a sentimentalist or a dolt; it had tended, and was still further tending, to make him the disciplined thinker and the high-minded and estimable man.

James Gardner was delighted throughout the voyage by the faithfulness of his friend to his augmented convictions of Christian duty. Bible-reading was his sacred habit, as also were private and social prayer. He dared not to be ashamed of Christ.

CHAPTER IV.

HAVELOCK IN BURMAH.

"HAVELOCK was a Christian—not as men now usually are, according a faint belief to the doctrines taught in childhood, but a man of the true old Puritan stamp, a man who really believed, and who, seeing the path of duty, held consequences as light as air. His piety underlaid his entire character. There could be but one path—that of duty; and therefore he was never indecisive. There could be but one object of fear—sin; and personal danger was as the idle wind. There could be but one who ruled—that was the Most High God; wherefore exultation and despondency were alike impossible." *

In this temper he landed with his regiment in India in 1823, determined from the first, as a solemn Christian duty, to devote his time and attention to the spiritual welfare of his men, and to assemble them together, as opportunity might be

* The *Friend of India.*

afforded, for reading the Scriptures and for devotional exercises.

"He also immediately sought out the men most distinguished in Calcutta for their piety, and amongst the rest the Rev. Mr Thomason, the chaplain of the Mission Church, who then stood with the foremost of all the good and godly in the metropolis."

This pleasant fellowship continued all the while he was in garrison at Fort William, the Scriptures opening to him in yet greater fulness, and his consecration to his Saviour's service assuming, as his associates gladly noticed, yet greater intelligence and force. With his men he was assiduous and discreet; the earnest exhorter always, but the exhorter who sought by kind persuasion to win them to the Lord Christ.

His endeavours never overlooked constitutional diversities, and he made all allowance for a man's bringing-up. He studied tempers carefully, and brought truth to bear upon individual minds in the best way he could, one by one. His religious influence over his men was remarkable; and though he was a strict disciplinarian, he gained their hearty goodwill.

In a narrative written by him of the occurrences of that time, he writes:—

"He was in garrison with his regiment at Fort William, Calcutta, when, in April 1824, war was declared against the Burmans. He was thereupon appointed to the general staff of Sir

Archibald Campbell as Deputy-Assistant-Adjutant-General at head-quarters. He proceeded to Rangoon, and took part in the actions near it. Thousands there fell victims to the climate, and, his health having been for the first time broken in upon by an attack of liver complaint, he was compelled to return, first to Calcutta, and then to Bombay and the Deccan."

"When I first knew Havelock, in 1824," a correspondent writes, "he was only eight-and-twenty; but he was conspicuous as an earnest student of his profession, a chivalrous soldier, and a man of the highest integrity. That which formed the brightest glory in his whole career was his sterling Christian consistency. He was not a man to parade his opinions or feelings, or to make any striking display, unless called for by some act or word of others, when no one could be more firm in the avowal of his sentiments, and his calm, impressive manner always told with effect."

The change of air, and the relaxation which he had obtained, had a most favourable effect in the restoration of his health. "He sailed back by Madras to Rangoon, found the army at Prome, and fought with it at Napadee, Patanago, and Pagham-Myo.

"On the conclusion of the peace at Yandabo, he was associated with Lieutenant-Colonel, then Captain Lumsden, of the Bengal Artillery, and with Dr Knox, of the Madras Army, in a mission to the

Burman capital at Ava, and they had audience of the monarch."

With the progress of these affairs in Burmah there were associated two individuals whom the Church of God delights to honour—the Rev. Dr and Mrs Judson, missionaries to the Burmese.

They had been in Burmah many years, and by their excellent character and conduct had been enabled to preach and teach without much molestation from the authorities. At the commencement of hostilities with the English, their liberty was at once abridged, and before long they were charged with being the spies of the British Government. Dr Judson was arrested and imprisoned at Ava, enduring for nearly two years indignities and sufferings that have rarely been equalled, never surpassed.

In her narrative of the imprisonment of her husband, Mrs Judson says :—" He was confined in the death prison with three pairs of iron fetters, and fastened to a long pole to prevent his moving." " The continual extortions and oppressions to which he is subject are indescribable." "Sometimes, for days and days together, I could not go into the prison till after dark, when I had two miles to walk in returning to the house. Oh, how many, many times have I returned from that dreary prison at nine o'clock at night, solitary and worn out with fatigue and anxiety." " It was at the commencement of the hot season. There were above a hundred prisoners shut up in one room, without a breath of air, except from a crack in the boards. I sometimes obtained permission to go to the door for five minutes, when my heart sickened at the wretchedness exhibited. The white prisoners, from incessant perspiration and loss of appetite, looked more like the dead than the living. I made daily application to the Governor, offering him money, which he refused."

An English officer, who had been taken prisoner by the Burmans, and imprisoned with Dr Judson, has thankful remembrance of these exertions of Mrs Judson :—

"She was the author of those eloquent and forcible appeals to the Government, which prepared them by degrees for submission to terms of peace, never expected by any who knew the *hauteur* and inflexible pride of the Burman Court. And while on this subject, the overflowings of grateful feelings compel me to add a tribute of public thanks to that amiable and humane lady, who, though living at a distance of two miles from the prison, and without any means of conveyance, and very feeble in health, forgot her own comfort and infirmity, and almost every day visited us, sought out, and administered to our wants, and contributed in every way to alleviate our misery.

"While we were all left by the Government destitute of food, she with unwearied perseverance, and by some means or other, obtained for us a constant supply.

"When the tattered state of our clothes evinced the extremity of our distress, she was ever ready to repair our scanty wardrobe.

"When the unfeeling avarice of our keepers confined us inside, or made our feet fast in the stocks, she, like a ministering angel, never ceased her applications to the Government, until she was authorised to communicate to us either the grateful news of our enlargement or of a respite from our galling oppressions.

"Besides all this, it was unquestionably owing in a chief degree to the forcible appeals of Mrs Judson, that the untutored Burman was finally made willing to secure the welfare and happiness of his country by a lasting peace."

Mrs Judson was the only white Christian female in Ava, and the only foreigner who was not consigned to prison. Her whole time, with the exception of twenty days, when she was confined by the birth of her child, was devoted to the alleviation of the sorrows of her husband and of his fellow-prisoners. Her perfect familiarity with the language of the country provided her with the means, and her superior manners and appearance often found her the opportunity, of addressing the officers of Government, which she did most assiduously, in the interests of peace.

Her biographer tells us, that the knowledge of her deeds had reached the British camp before the conclusion of hostilities. She was received at the camp at Yandaboo, with such honours as would have been paid to a lady of the most exalted rank. Sir Archibald Campbell, the Commander-in-Chief, treated her with parental kindness, and everything the army could command was made to minister to her comfort.

On the conclusion of hostilities, a dinner was given by General Campbell to the Burmese Commissioners, at which Mrs Judson was invited to be present. The scene, which Havelock witnessed, is thus described by Dr Judson :—

"When the dinner hour arrived, the company marched in couples to the music of the band toward the table, led by the General, who walked alone. As they came opposite to the tent with the verandah before it, suddenly the music ceased, the whole procession stood still; and, while the wondering Burmans turned their eyes in all directions, the General entered the tent. In a moment he reappeared with a lady on his arm,—no stranger to the conscious Commissioners,—whom he led to the table, and seated at his own right hand.

"The abashed Commissioners slid into their seats shrinkingly, where they sat as though transfixed by a mixture of astonishment and fear.

"'I fancy,' General Campbell remarked, 'these gentleman must be old acquaintances of yours, Mrs Judson; and, judging from their appearance, you must have used them very ill.'

"Mrs Judson smiled. The Burmans could not

understand the remark, but considered themselves the subject of it evidently, and their faces were blank with consternation.

"'What is the matter with yonder owner of the pointed beard?' pursued Sir Archibald, 'he seems to be seized with an ague fit.'

"'I do not know,' answered Mrs Judson, fixing her eyes on the trembler, 'unless his memory may be too busy. He is an old acquaintance of mine, and may probably infer danger to himself from seeing me under your protection.'"

The fact was, that of the most barbarous of her husband's oppressors, this very man was the chief. To herself personally his behaviour had been cruel in the extreme. On Mrs Judson's reciting this at the table, expressions of indignation burst from the listening officers. The man became obviously alarmed at the intimations of their anger, and only when Mrs Judson, addressing him in an under tone in Burmese, assured him he had nothing to fear, was he at all composed. Even then it was clear to everybody that he was ill at ease.

"I never thought," remarked Dr Judson, when he told the story, "that I was over and above vindictive; but really it was one of the richest scenes I ever beheld."

And there sat Havelock amongst the British officers, joining both in their expressions of indignation against the man who had perpetrated such barbarities, and in their respectful and chivalrous indications of admiration towards the missionaries of Jesus by whom they had been so heroically endured.

That instance of moral heroism was not without effect on him just then. He had to bear a good deal of scorn on account of his religious habits. The trial of his faith was somewhat sharp. Only press him hard enough, it was sometimes supposed, and he would give his Methodism to the winds. It was a mean and miserable thing, of which brave men ought to be heartily ashamed!

Dr Judson had some claim to the character of a brave man. And what had made him brave, but conscious reliance upon God's power, and personal assurance of an interest in God's love? The trust that Havelock endeavoured to put in a special providence Judson had been exercising when in his horrid dungeon at Oung-pen-la. The habit which the Lieutenant was maintaining of daily fellowship with God was the very habit which had constituted the missionary a man of celebrity and renown. His companions in arms admired their evangelical visitor; they could, therefore, hardly hold their evangelical comrade in contempt.

During his sojourn in Rangoon, Havelock kept up his practice of assembling his men for religious worship and instruction. He was also busily occupied in holding back the soldiers from the excesses to which, in a captured city, there were so many strong inducements. Abstemious himself, if not altogether an abstainer from alcoholic beverages, he went about imploring the men to keep clear of intemperance. "There is no such soldier in the world," he used to say, "as the English soldier, if he can be kept from drink." And, believing that the strength of Christian principle was the only effectual safeguard against the evil, he laboured to bring it into existence and operation. He would warn and encourage, as best he could, leaving it with God to give the blessing.

There is in Rangoon a famous heathen temple devoted to the service of Boodh, and known as "The Magnificent Shway-dagong" pagoda. It is deemed the glory of the city. Of a chamber in this building Havelock obtained possession for his own purposes. All around the place were small images of Boodh, in the usual position, sitting with their legs gathered up and crossed, and the hands resting on the lap in symbol and expression of repose. No great alterations were necessary for the purposes of Christian service. Abominable idolatries had been witnessed there beyond all doubt, but no sacerdotal purifications were requisite ere adoration of the true God, and service well-pleasing to Him, could be offered through Jesus Christ. Havelock remembered well that "neither in this mountain nor yet at Jerusalem" were men to worship the Father now. To the true worshippers any place might become a place for worship. Even the pagoda of Shway-dagong might be none other than the house of God and the gate of heaven.

Accordingly it was announced that that would be the place of religious meeting. An officer relates that as he was wandering round the pagoda on one occasion, he heard the sound, strange enough as he thought, of singing. He listened, and found that it was certainly psalm singing. He determined to follow the sound to its source, and started for the purpose. At length he reached the chamber, and what should meet his eye but Havelock with his Bible and hymn-book before him, and more than a hundred men seated around him giving earnest heed to his proclamation to them of the glad tidings of great joy. How had they got the light by which to read, for the place was in dark shade? They had obtained lamps for the purpose, and putting them in order, had lit them and placed them one by one in an idol's lap. There they were, those dumb but significant lamp-bearers, in constant use; and they were there, we may be well assured, to suggest stirring thoughts to the Lieutenant and his men. How well the 115th Psalm would be understood there! How impressively some parts of the first chapter of the Romans would be explained! How earnestly the prayer would be offered that the Burmese might be induced, through the power of the Holy Ghost, to cast these and all other idols to the moles and to the bats! How gratefully would thanksgiving be offered that He who is our God is the God of salvation, the God and Father of our Lord Jesus Christ!

Havelock was practically anxious about the heathen and their salvation. With the men whose especial object it was to preach the gospel to the natives, and to translate the sacred Scriptures into the vernaculars of India, he had great sympathy. Whoever might despise them, and counsel their dismissal, at any risk he took their part. It was, after all, not by the sword that India could be retained. Unless a moral and religious influence could be propagated, well was he assured that our dominion there must ultimately lick the dust. He gave therefore to Bible and Missionary Societies all the countenance and succour within his power. If his addresses at their meetings could aid them, they could always command him. If he could employ his pen on their behalf, it was at their service. If pecuniary contributions were required, he was ready to subscribe.

His mode of doing this was noticeable. Early in his religious life he came under the strong conviction that to the Lord's service there was due at least one tenth of his income. There was nothing servile at all, or in anywise uncongenial in this conviction. Not in the spirit of bondage did he yield to it, but in the spirit of adoption ; purposing in his heart as a cheerful giver that at any rate he would set apart as much as that. Even from the slender income of a subaltern, and when domestic claims were increasing year by year, that proportion was "sacredly devoted to thé objects of Christian benevolence."

No godliness of mere psalm-singing was Havelock's. It is told that whilst in Burmah, the army was one day suddenly apprised of the near approach of the enemy. Sir Archibald Campbell sent in great haste to order the men of a particular corps to occupy at once a prescribed post. Imminent as was the danger, the order was to no purpose, for the men of that regiment were so many of them intoxicated that it was unfit for duty. The position was embarrassing, and would presently have become serious. The General knew this well, and he knew, too, upon whom he could depend in such an emergency. "Then," said he, "call out Havelock's saints; they are never drunk, and Havelock is always ready." The bugle sounded; they were immediately under arms, the enemy was repulsed, and the General's object achieved.

Though not intended to be complimentary, either to the officer or to his men, the epithet was just the one which described, if not all his men, yet the officer himself. In opposition, alike to the sanctimonious and the profane, he had willed to live godly in Christ Jesus. It was a cool, calm, well-considered determination; and how well he adhered to it, under most testing circumstances, a brother-officer has described:—"He invariably secured two hours in the morning for reading the Scriptures and private prayer. If the march began at six he rose at four; if at four he rose at two." Time he must have, and time he obtained, for being alone with

God. Then it was that he put on the whole armour of God afresh, and renewed his strength. In this way he was anointed with fresh oil, finding to his glad experience, that the secret of the Lord was with him, and that He shewed to him his covenant. In his closet he girded up the loins of his mind, and reassured himself that whether he lived, he lived to the Lord, or whether he died, he died unto the Lord —that whether living or dying, he was the Lord's. And never was our Saviour's promise more signally verified than in his case. God our Father, who seeth in secret, when we have retired to pray, promises to reward us openly. What but an open rewarding was the grace which was given to Havelock for the adorning the doctrine of God his Saviour in all things?

CHAPTER V.

HAVELOCK'S FRAGMENTARY MEMORANDA FROM 1827 TO 1849.

THESE twenty-two years of Havelock's life were eventful in the extreme. In the active service in which he was engaged the sincerity of his religion was exposed continually to the severest tests, but through every vicissitude he held fast his profession of faith in the providence and grace of God.

He consented one day to jot down his reminiscences of that period, contenting himself, however, with a few lines in relation to each year. Written, as they were, by himself, it has been deemed desirable to give them *verbatim*, with such amplifications from his letters, and other sources of information, as may be necessary for shewing their connexion with his most active life, and their bearing on his religious character :—

"1827. *Rejoined Regiment at Dinapore, and was soon after appointed by Lord Combermere, Adjutant to the depôt of King's troops at Chinsurah.*"

"*Commenced publication of 'Memoirs of Campaign in Ava.'*"

"1828. *Published the 'Memoirs' by subscription, in the intervals of professional exertions at Chinsurah.*"

The opportunities which the Burmese war gave to Havelock, to test by actual experience the principles of military science and strategy with which he had early made himself acquainted, were not thrown away; and, though still only a subaltern, he prepared and published by subscription his "Memoir of the three Campaigns." But to little purpose had he launched on the perilous sea of authorship. In the preface to his "War in Affghanistan," he says, with a dash of regret:—"My former effort as an author had not met with that species of reward which is commonly looked for at the present day. No enterprising publisher had taken under his auspices my 'Memoir of the three Campaigns.' It had been printed in a distant land, and thus placed beyond the reach of the praise or blame of the constituted critics of Britain; and in consequence of the short memories of a large proportion of my subscribers, the proceeds of the publication had scarcely defrayed the cost of giving it to a limited number of readers. Yet a counterpoise to these mortifications was not wanting. A few officers of rank, whose discernment and candour I could not doubt, even in my own cause, had characterised the performance as honest and faithful; three Commanders-in-Chief in India had spoken favourably of it to others as well as to myself; and I have been deceived if, when war was likely to be renewed in the Burman Empire, and information regarding it had again become valuable, a fourth General, placed in the same situation of responsible control above adverted to, did not find, or profess to find, in the pages of the neglected Lieutenant, developments of fact and reasoning which he had in vain sought in books on the same topic that had enjoyed the sunshine of a far more brilliant popularity."

"1829. *February 9th, Anniversary of Fight at Pagham-Myo. Married at Serampore to Hannah, the third daughter of Dr Marshman.*"

Of this marriage it may be said, that a happier one was never celebrated. No wish entertained by their friends on the wedding morning seems to have been unfulfilled; except, indeed, that which desired their residence together continuously to the end of life. The privilege of reciprocal and devoted attachment was theirs through a union of more than twenty-eight years. A characteristic anecdote is told by Mr Marshman. "Havelock had been summoned to attend a court-martial on the morning appointed for the wedding. Instead of sending an excuse, he thought it his duty to go down to Calcutta, and proceeded from the altar to the boat. Having completed his duty as a member of the court, he returned to the wedding-feast in the evening."

"1830. *Depôt moved to Fort William by Lord William Bentinck at the latter end of the year.*"

"*April 4. Havelock baptized at Serampore by the Rev. John Mack, having since walked ever with the Baptists.*"

In reference to this incident in his religious history, and to the consistency with which he subsequently acted, it has been said, "He was not a large or liberal-minded man; on the contrary, he was a sectarian of the Baptist persuasion." If by sectarianism be intended attachment to a particular body of Christians, then this witness, of course, is true; but if, as the critic intimates, sectarianism, in the sense of narrowmindedness and censoriousness, distinguished him, then his witness about Havelock is not true.

As a soldier he was a sectarian, in that he served immediately with the 13th Light Infantry; but then he was not a sectarian, by refusing to serve with any soldier not of the 13th. By association with a particular military corps, he did not dissociate himself from the main body of the British forces. His regiment was a sect, in the sense of being one part of the whole; it was not a sect in keeping aloof from or in decrying the chivalrous and heroic doings of every other part. Havelock belonged, no doubt, to the 13th; but then it was through the 13th that he belonged to the army at large. His regimental attachments notwithstanding, he was known as the large and liberal-minded comrade of every soldier, whether of the company or of the Queen.

It was just thus with him religiously. He

worked immediately with one section of the Church, but he was ever ready to work with any who were the disciples of his Saviour. A speech made by him at Bombay, as recently as 1849, exactly puts the course which from the first he habitually pursued. Having stated his denominational preferences, he said :—

"But whilst he should part with his Baptist principles only with his life, he declared his willingness cordially to fraternise with every Christian who held by the Head, and was serving the Redeemer in sincerity and truth. And here he would protest against its being alleged, as adversaries would insinuate, that where men of various denominations met, as this evening, in a feeling of brotherhood, they could only do this, by paring down to the smallest portion the mass of their religion ; on the contrary, he conceived that all brought with them their faith in all its strength and vitality. They left, indeed, he thought, at the door of the place of assembly the husks and shell of their creed, but brought into the midst of their brethren the precious kernel. They laid aside, for a moment, at the threshold, the canons, and articles, and formularies, of their section of Christianity ; but carried along with them, up to the table at which he was speaking, the very essence and quintessence of their religion."

The juxtaposition of Havelock's baptism with his introduction to the family of the Rev. Dr Marshman has led to the opinion, in some quarters, that it was in this way his denominational preferences were originated. The opinion is a mistaken one. He assured his sister that on his voyage to India, on board the "General Kyd," in the early part of 1823, he had formed the convictions on which afterwards he acted at Serampore.

"1831. *Establishment at Chinsurah abolished. Rejoined Regiment at Dinapore, and commenced a series of religious instruction to the Baptist soldiers of the* 13*th. The Church in the Regiment at one time numbered about thirty men and women.*"

His object was not to proselytise. To any one who chose to take advantage of the religious instruction which he provided, it was thrown wide open. No proof was necessary of a man's being "a Baptist soldier," before he could be allowed to join in the praise and prayer and instruction of their assembly. Every man in the regiment was welcome. But the design not being to sectarianise, the Lieutenant left their coming or their staying away entirely free.

"1832. *Regiment marched to Agra, where the Baptist soldiers rebuilt a chapel, in which there was a pastor and a considerable congregation, when Havelock revisited it with Sir Hugh Gough in* 1843.

"1833. *Passed examination in native languages before Station Committee at Agra, and went down to Calcutta for examination at the College of Fort-William. Instruction of the Baptist soldiers blessed with much success.*"

The intellectual discipline to which he had attained, and the knowledge he had acquired under his venerated tutor Dr Raine, at the Charter House, came greatly to his help now. The discipline had been yet further matured, and the knowledge continually augmented, so that he was found thoroughly competent—the accomplished and well-furnished man.

Between whiles, he prosecuted his course of teaching his men in the name of Jesus Christ—going from Boards of Examiners to prayer-meetings; blending in his daily occupations the solution of hard questions in philology with exhortations to repent of sin, and to believe in Christ. He had time, too, to inquire into the effects of his exhortations; thanking God for blessing him, at the same time, as the evangelist and the oriental scholar.

"1834. *Passed examination in languages at College of Fort-William. Appointed Acting-Interpreter to 16th Foot, stationed at Cawnpore. Family residing at Cherra-Poongee for recovery of health.*"

"1835. *Appointed Adjutant of the 13th Light Infantry, and rejoined it at Agra, under Colonel Sale.*"

About this appointment to the adjutancy of his own regiment, there arose great difficulties on account of his religious habits. He had neither concealed nor compromised his convictions of the preeminent importance of the fear of God. He had aimed to stand fast in the liberty with which Christ had made him free. Desiring to be as courteous as any officer in the army, he had striven to be conscientious withal. Happy for him it was that his faith, as well as the faith of his religious associates, had shewed itself by its good works.

Application had been made on Havelock's behalf to Lord William Bentinck for the vacant situation. His lordship made not the slightest objection on any professional ground. To every question touching his fitness for the post, the answer was satisfactory in the extreme; but there were objections. To shew this, bundles of letters were exhibited by Lord William, written avowedly to prevent such a fanatic and enthusiast as Havelock from obtaining what, at that time, was his highest ambition. Still, the application was respectfully, but earnestly pressed,—so earnestly as it could have been only by one who was the best of all acquainted both with his anxieties and with his claims. "There is no reflection on his courage, or on his loyalty, or on his moral character?" "Not the least." "Then must he be sacrificed," asked Mrs Havelock, "to the prejudices of the irreligious and the profane?" There was a little delay, and then came the appointment that had been so well solicited, but so bitterly opposed; and it came, because, as the Governor-General declared, "he was the fittest man for it."

To see whether the complaints against Havelock

were really of any weight, this had been done. A Return was ordered of the offences committed by the men in the different companies, and the punishment inflicted on them ; and it was found that the men of Havelock's company, and those who joined them in their religious exercises, were the most sober and the best behaved in the regiment. "The complaint is," said the Governor-General, "that they are Baptists; I only wish that the whole regiment was Baptist."

Not unlike the case of Daniel was the case of Havelock just now. No occasion could be found against him, except it could be found against him concerning the law of his God. And when that came to be investigated, it turned out that the men who feared God were the men who honoured the king. The praying soldiers were the soldiers who had not deserved punishment. The fanatics were those who kept themselves away from the canteen. The enthusiasts were "the most sober and the best behaved" of all their comrades. "The saints," by that most faithful of all tests—an official military Return—were the honour and the safety of the regiment in which they served.

"1836. *Regiment marched to Kurnal. Baptist soldiers built a chapel there. Family resided at Landour, where their bungalow was reduced to ashes. A little girl, and two servants, lost their lives in the fire, and Mrs Havelock was dreadfully burnt. Recovered, by God's mercy, after being six weeks confined to her couch.*"

A beautiful incident occurred in connexion with this calamity, which is thus communicated:—

"A few months after the birth of his little daughter his faith was greatly tried by a fearful domestic calamity. His wife and youthful family had been sent up to Landour, in the Himalayas, for change of air. A few days before their intended return to him, it was so ordained that on a calm, bright moonlight night, when not a breath of air stirred a leaf, the cry of 'fire!' was suddenly heard, and the thatched bungalow or cottage which contained all that on earth was dearest to the Christian soldier, was enwrapped in flames. And though the family were, partly by their own exertions, and partly by the aid of friends and their servants, rescued from the devouring element, it was not before the infant daughter had been so burnt that she died a few days after; and the mother, in rescuing her boys, was so much injured that it was years before she recovered her former health.

"With what feelings did the God-fearing man receive the intelligence by the next morning's post, from a brother officer, that his wife and child were lying at the point of death,—his loved wife, from whom he had heard only the day before that she hoped in a few days to return to her happy home to present him his three children in robust health? He bowed meekly to the will of his God. And how did the regiment receive the tidings? The men came in a body to their Adjutant, begging him to allow each man to devote one month's pay, to help him to sustain the loss of property. This, of course, he declined, but it shewed the high estimation in which he was held by his men."

When this account reached him, he was at table with his brother-officers; and his distress was overpowering. He had been away with his regiment for some time. At the earliest moment he hastened to sympathise with his wife under the loss of their darling child, and to render her such help as might be within his power. Letters, written by him at the time, indicate the amount of danger which threatened Mrs Havelock's life, and also his devoted and self-denying solicitude for her recovery. It seemed as though he could nurse in a sick chamber quite as well as he could pass examinations at Fort William, or take and keep his position in the field. He was most assiduous and considerate during the suspense of those anxious six weeks, alternating between hope and fear, as his letters testify; but trusting in God's mercy throughout, that he should be spared the impending blow. Grateful are the reminiscences now of that period of deep affliction, when the father and the husband turned to such good account the exceeding great and precious promises of the grace of God. The Lord had given that child: the Lord had taken it away. Should they not, mother and father together, say, Blessed be the name of the Lord?

"*Received the intelligence of my father's death at Exeter in his eightieth year.*"

"1837. *Adjutant of regiment at Kurnal. Continued religious instruction to soldiers, and did something to promote temperance habits among them. Dr Marshman's happy death at Serampore.*"

Havelock's promotion to the adjutancy had not diminished his desire to do good, and to communicate, to the men under his command. He took care not to trench upon the duties of other persons, but obligations were laid on him to inculcate wherever he could the claims of temperance, and integrity, and godliness. It was often up-hill work, especially when, instead of co-operation from his equals and superiors, some of them did all within their power to bring his exertions into contempt.

Against opposition from highest quarters Havelock held quietly on his way, remembering that what God's grace had done for himself, that also it could do for every other man on earth. Drunkenness was a nuisance as well as a sin; he determined to check it if he could. Irreligion was a disgrace to any profession; he would work away against irreligiousness, depending on the Holy Spirit of promise for making men willing in the day of God's power.

It will be noted that "Dr Marshman's happy death" is expressly mentioned in these memoranda. Never did his son-in-law omit a reference to that venerable man when the opportunity occurred. His connexion with the doctor's family had been a growing occasion to him of the purest satisfaction, and it was a source of pleasure to him to the last that his eldest son, Henry Marshman Havelock, bore its honoured name.

"1838. *Promoted to a Captaincy* AFTER SERVING TWENTY-THREE YEARS AS A SUBALTERN *officer. Army formed to invade Affghanistan. Appointed Aide-de-Camp to Sir Willoughby Cotton. Marched to the point of assembling at Ferozepore, and commenced advance down the Indus.*"

The attention of Government had for some time been directed to certain Russian emissaries in Affghanistan, who were known to be assiduously cultivating friendly relations for the Czar with the warlike Affghan chiefs. To counteract their influence, it was considered desirable that proposals of friendly alliance should be made on the part of the British to Dost Mohammed Khan, who, at that time, held Cabool with a considerable army. These overtures were declined. The necessity for immediate action was thus made evident. "Matters had reached a crisis," wrote Havelock. "The character and object of the views and combinations of Russia herself could no longer be questioned by the most imbecile, the most interested, or the most sceptical amongst us; they were fully unmasked. Not to mention the intrigues, of which Cabool and Candahar were at this very moment the scene, an endeavour had now openly been made to establish for Persia, that is, by the juggling processes of Sclavonic transmutation, for the Czar himself, a place of arms within one hundred marches of the Indus at Attock.

"The remedy proposed by the Governor-General of India was not, as some might have advised, to assume the line of the Indus in a defensive manner, and await on its left bank the further development of the projects of our secret and declared enemies; but boldly to pass that boundary, and achieve at once a total change in the aspect of affairs beyond it, by dethroning the Barukzye rulers, and reinstating in the possession of a part of the dominions of his father, and his grandfather, that Shooja-ool-Moolk, with whom Elphinstone had journeyed to Peshawur to treat, when the genius of Napoleon had thirty years before taught us to tremble in the expectation of another form of aggressive violence. The day of calamity of this prince had then commenced; for since that period he had lingered in exile, eating the idle bread of dependence, or in his bolder and more active mood wearying himself in fruitless intrigues and efforts to recover his lost empire, evincing, amidst a series of repulses and disappointments, all the perseverance of a De Medici, a Stuart, or a Bourbon."

To replace this prince upon the throne of his fathers was the object of the expedition which was this year despatched to Affghanistan, under the command of Sir John Fane.

"1839. *Marched to Bhawulpore. Fort Bukkur*

surrendered. Marched into Scinde. Retraced our steps and crossed the Indus. Occupied Kandahar. Stormed Ghuznee. Marched to Cabool. Moved down to Jellalabad and Peshawur with Sir Willoughby Cotton. Obtained leave to return to India to prepare for publication my account of the campaign."

The expedition was formed chiefly from the army of Bengal, together with a column from Bombay, under the command of Sir John Keane. As the route of the Bengal force necessarily lay through the Sikh States, a political interview, with its usual accompaniments of military display, took place at Ferozepore between the Governor-General and our ally, Runjeet Singh. From thence the force, lessened in number in consequence of the siege of Herat, which had been invested by Persia under Russian influence, being raised, advanced on Affghanistan through the territories of the lesser Sikh States.

Sir John Fane having here resigned the chief command of the expedition, the Bengal contingent advanced under the command of Sir Willoughby Cotton to the town of Dadur, having obtained possession of the important fortress of Bukkur on the way. Skirting the desert of Cutch Gandava, Sir Willoughby traversed the pass of the Bolan, a mountain defile more than 5000 feet above the sea-level, and grand in its naked desolation, through which, though led to expect opposition, the Affghan chiefs suffered the army to pass unmolested. From this point he advanced on Kwettah, through a country sterile, barren, and almost destitute of water. At Kwettah Sir John Keane, having joined the army with the Bombay column, assumed the chief command. Leaving this place on the 7th of March, the force, now joined by Shah Shooja and his army, advanced by distressing marches—their sufferings greatly increased by the heat and want of food and water—till, on the 27th of April, Sir John Keane occupied, without resistance, the ancient city of Candahar, the western capital of Affghanistan. Here he seated the Shah on the throne of his ancestors.

On the 27th of June the army began its advance upon Cabool, accompanied by the Shah Shooja in person. As the force drew near to Ghuznee, deemed by the Affghans to be impregnable, and standing right in his way, Sir John Keane found the enemy determined to dispute his passage. Unable to breach the walls, having left his siege guns behind at Candahar, he resolved that the gate of the fortress should be blown in. After a determined resistance, Havelock, who had been actively employed, saw the colours of his own regiment waving on its tower. "Thus," he writes, "was Ghuznee lost and won; thus, in little more than two short hours, a garrison, plausibly estimated at 3500 men, was dispossessed of a fortress, the walls of which, up to the moment of attack, had scarcely been grazed by cannon shot, the fire of the works being as entire as in the first hour of investment. This had been done without a ladder being raised in escalade. . . .

"Let it be recorded to the honour of the captors, that though Ghuznee was carried by storm, after a resistance stout enough to have roused the angry passions of the assailants, the Affghans were everywhere spared when they ceased to fight; and it is in itself a moral triumph exceeding in value and duration the praise of the martial achievement of the troops, that, in a fortress captured by assault, not the slightest insult was offered to one of the females found in the zenana within the walls of the citadel.

"This forbearance, and these substantive proofs of excellent discipline, reflect more credit on officers and men than the indisputable skill and valour displayed in the operation. But let me not be accused of foisting in unfairly a favourite topic, or attempting to detract from the merit of the troops, when I remark in how great a degree the self-denial, mercy, and generosity of the hour may be attributed to the fact of the European soldiers having received no spirit ration since the 8th of July, and having found no intoxicating liquor amongst the plunder of Ghuznee. No candid man of any military experience will deny that the character of the scene in the fortress and citadel would have been far different if individual soldiers had entered the town primed with arrack, or if spirituous liquors had been discovered in the Affghan depots. Since then, it has been proved that troops can make forced marches of forty miles,* and storm a fortress in seventy-five minutes, without the aid of rum, behaving, after success, with a forbearance and humanity unparalleled in history; let it not henceforth be argued that distilled spirits are an indispensable portion of a soldier's ration. The medical officers of this army have distinctly attributed to their previous abstinence from strong drink the rapid recovery of the wounded at Ghuznee."

Dost Mohammed was not slow to perceive that in the fall of Ghuznee he had lost, not only his prestige, but his chief fortress. He therefore despatched his brother to negotiate terms of surrender of the crown of Cabool to the Shah. But as he refused to reside under British surveillance, his offer was declined. Abandoned by his army, he fled to the mountains, leaving his artillery to be captured on the road. Hajee Khan, who had made submission to the Shah Shooja, volunteered to effect his capture with 2000 Affghans, and Major Outram, "one of the most resolute, intelligent, and active officers in the British army," says Havelock, "was well selected to command Dost Mohammed's pursuers." Outram had with him a small, but active, body of horse. His pursuit was bold, resolute, and persevering. He followed the Ameer in hot pursuit over an arid tract, and up tre-

* The 4th Brigade and General Willshire's column had to march this distance in order to join head quarters, previously to the attack of Ghuznee.

mendous passes, but foiled by the defection of Hajee Khan, he returned to the camp unsuccessful.

The advance of the army on Cabool was not further disputed, and on the 8th of May the Shah Shooja was formally crowned there with every circumstance of pomp and external honour, but, it could not be concealed, with little welcome from his people.

The object of the expedition having been accomplished, General Keane prepared to return to Bombay, leaving behind, to insure the stability of the Shah's position in Cabool, a considerable portion of the troops he had conducted there; Sir William MacNaghten and Sir Alexander Burnes—the former an old school-companion of Havelock's at the Charterhouse,—remaining as envoy and political agent at the Court of the Shah.

Crossing the Khoord Cabool pass, they reached Jellalabad, from which another march brought them to Peshawur. Here Havelock and his fellow-officers enjoyed the boundless hospitality of General Avitabili, a Neapolitan in the service of Runjeet Singh, who held that important fortress for the Maharajah. In after years, he often alluded to the Persian couplet, inscribed over the door of his dining-room, to which, amidst this scene of festivity, the Neapolitan General pointed his attention, that "The morning might begin with a bright sun, and yet the evening be darkened with storms," to illustrate the mutability of human affairs. Two years after,

Havelock entered the same room, after the destruction of 13,000 men in the passes, and the loss of our prestige in Affghanistan and Central Asia, and his host again pointed to these memorable lines.

"1840. *Returned to India through the Punjaub. Made the acquaintance of Ventura, Court, and the other foreign officers in the army of Kurruch Sing at Lahore. Proceeded to Serampore, and sent off my Memoir for publication in India. Placed in command of detachments, and returned by the Ganges to Ferozepore. Accompanied General Elphinstone's escort and convoy back to Cabool.*"

The Memoir referred to will long remain a lasting monument of the military science and brilliant genius of its author; and it will awaken, too, a regret that the same pen had not given to the world a narrative as complete, of the subsequent campaigns in which he took so distinguished a part.

In the meantime, indications had not been wanting that the British troops would soon be needed to maintain the throne of the Shah. Reinforcements were accordingly sent to Cabool, under the command of General Elphinstone, to whom, on his arrival, Sir Willoughby Cotton resigned the chief command, and prepared to return to India.

During the vicissitudes of this year Havelock's efforts as an evangelist among the soldiers were most diligently pursued, specially with those of the detachments whom he had officially in charge. A friend, passing through Cabool at this time, attended one of the meetings of the congregation of soldiers, and stated to Mr Marshman that he should never forget the thrilling sensation he felt in that romantic position, while the men stood up and sang with heart and soul the 100th Psalm, as Havelock gave out the words—

> "Ye nations round the earth, rejoice
> Before the Lord, your sovereign King;
> Serve Him with cheerful heart and voice,
> With all your tongues His glories sing."

"When the friend who was present heard soon after of the glorious defence of Jellalabad by these troops and their comrades, his mind involuntarily reverted to the little band of Christian soldiers surrounding Havelock in the room at Cabool, and he thought that men thus nerved with the vigour of Christian principle and devotion were prepared to face any enemy, and to overcome any difficulty."

"1841. *Appointed Persian interpreter to General Elphinstone. Eastern Ghilzies rise and blockade Cabool. Sent to the camp of Sir Robert Sale, and present at the forcing of Khoord Cabool Pass. Return with despatches to Cabool. Again despatched to Sir Robert's camp, who, after the affairs at Tezeen, detains me with his force, which moved on, every day engaged with the enemy, to Gundamuck. Receive intelligence of the insurrection at Cabool, and fall back on Jellalabad. The memorable defence commences.*"

It had become daily evident to every one but the

political agents that Cabool was on the eve of a fearful outbreak. The efforts of the British to maintain the authority of the Shah could not be otherwise than detestable to those hordes of mountain banditti who lived by plunder and rapine:—"I should define," wrote Havelock at the time, "the whole affair to be a struggle of the chiefs to maintain their power to misrule, of which they dreaded the annihilation; of certain tribes, especially the Eastern Ghilzies, to revenge the wrong of the reduction of their stipends; and, finally, of the whole people to get rid of the Feringhees. The facts are, that Sir Robert Sale's brigade, with its auxiliaries, having been moved down towards Tezeen and Gundamuck, with the double purpose of forcing the passes and returning to the provinces, that opportunity was seized to spring the mine. Sir A. Burnes was assassinated, with all our adherents, at Cabool, and our troops driven, by the force of a general insurrection, to confine their efforts to maintain themselves in the two points of the Bala-Hissar and the entrenched cantonment. This they are as yet successfully doing, and I trust, by God's blessing, will continue to do, until reinforcements arrive."

General Sale, at the head of the troops returning to India, had left Cabool early in October, the 13th, Havelock's regiment, forming part of his column. At the Khoord Cabool pass the enemy fiercely disputed his advance, and he found it necessary to send Havelock to communicate his difficulty to head-quarters. The answer received gave him to understand that he must chiefly rely upon his own efforts to achieve the passage. For eighteen days this gallant force fought its way, in spite of every obstacle, through a succession of dreary mountain passes,—above them and on either side nothing but granite peaks, on which not a blade of grass would grow,—all the while exhibiting an amount of patient endurance and sober restraint that told well the effect of their officers' example. Fighting their way, at length they reached Jellalabad.

Sir Robert Sale perceived at once that it would be madness to attempt with his present force the Khyber pass, which he must now penetrate to reach Peshawur. He, therefore, determined to take possession of Jellalabad, put it into a state of defence, and wait till he should be relieved. Few such chapters are to be found in the history of surmounted difficulties as the defence which now began.

Under the direction of Havelock's bosom friend, Captain George Broadfoot, the dilapidated defences were repaired, officers and men working away, with tools in one hand and sword in the other, night and day, with hardly any intermission, for a long six weeks. On the completion of the works, about Christmas-day, Havelock suggested to General Sale to assemble the whole garrison for the purpose of offering up thanks to Almighty God, "who had in His mercy enabled them to complete the fortifications necessary for their protection."

The suggestion was approved, and the necessary command given. There stood those brave-hearted and hard-handed men, awaiting the direction that might come next. "Let us pray," said Havelock's well-known voice. And at once before the presence of the great God those soldiers reverently bowed the knee, whilst at the impulse of a devout and grateful heart he poured forth supplication and praise in the name of the great High Priest—"Blessed be the Lord, my strength, which teacheth my hands to war and my fingers to fight. My goodness and my fortress: my high tower and my deliverer: my shield and he in whom I trust."

"1842. *Defence continued. Havelock commands the right column in the first attack on Mohammed Akbar's camp, for which he is afterwards promoted to majority by Brevet, and receives the Cross of Companion of the Bath. After General Pollock had forced the Khyber, Havelock is first nominated his interpreter, and afterwards appointed Deputy-Assistant-Adjutant-General to the Infantry Division. The army reoccupies Cabool. Havelock present at the fights at Mamoo Keil and Tezeen. Accompanies the force under Sir John M'Caskill into the Kohistan. Capture of Istaliffe. Army returns through the Khyber, where part of the Division of Infantry meets with disaster. The defenders of Jellalabad received with distinguished honours by Lord Ellenborough at Ferozepore.*"

Rumours of disasters in Cabool had been rife

during the siege, but if any trustworthy information had reached General Sale, he kept it to himself. On the 18th of January a solitary horseman was seen approaching the garrison, wounded, and scarcely able to sit his horse, grasping convulsively the hilt and a small fragment of a sword, which had been broken in the terrible conflict from which he had come. He proved to be Dr Brydon, and he believed himself to be the last survivor of General Elphinstone's army! His story confirmed their worst fears. More than 13,000 men, endeavouring to fight their way from Cabool, had perished miserably, either by Affghan bullets or among the snows of the Khoord Cabool!

February passed anxiously away, but it brought no relief to the beleaguered garrison. They were now in great straits for food and ammunition. An earthquake, destroying in one fearful night the labour of months, had added to their horrors. March wore on, and still no relief. Famine stared them in the face. General Pollock was still detained mysteriously at Peshawur, while Akbar Khan in great force maintained an effectual blockade.

Their condition at last became desperate, and as surrender was out of the question, early in April they determined to hazard everything on a final effort to break through the enemy's lines, and cut their way to Peshawur or perish in the attempt.

On the morning of the 7th, three columns, each 500 strong, issued from the garrison, one of them led by Havelock. They were accompanied by six guns, and a small but heroic squadron of horse. Though numbering many thousands, the enemy could not stand before them. Havelock's division, after a short but fierce struggle, turned his line, and, being promptly joined by the other columns, they made a simultaneous charge upon the flying foe, and completed his entire discomfiture. The guns then opened with tremendous effect; and, had their cavalry been in sufficient strength, very few of the hosts of Akbar Khan would have survived to tell the tale. Never was victory more complete. The spoil was very great, and when Sir George Pollock reached Jellalabad a few days afterwards, instead of finding a starving garrison, he found them masters of the position, and with food in abundance.

In August the "army of retribution" advanced upon Cabool. At the formidable pass of Tezeen, Akbar Khan, with 15,000 men, disputed their passage; but British valour was irresistible, and he gave way. His loss was great. Disappointed and powerless he fled to the mountains, leaving the passage to the capital free, where in a few days the English flag once more waved upon its battlements.

Sir George Pollock having learned that Akbar Khan with his retainers had retreated into Kohistan, and that he and his confederate chiefs were established in force at the mountain fortress of Istaliffe, determined to dislodge them. This was effected with great gallantry; and it is no longer a matter of question that to Havelock's strategic skill the success of this difficult operation was mainly owing.

General Sale had now the happiness of receiving back from their long captivity his wife and daughter, while Havelock was able to share his gratification in welcoming to liberty his own nephew, of whom nothing had been heard for many months. "As the relieved captives came up before the Cabool garrison, he inquired whether Lieutenant Henry Marshman Williams was among them: on which a tall, gaunt figure, with a beard of a twelvemonth's growth, and a sheepskin over his shoulders, stepped forward, and said, 'Here I am, uncle.' By his side stood the late chivalrous General Nicholson, then his junior in the regiment, whose name has since been immortalised by the capture of Delhi."

Having razed the fortifications of Cabool, and leaving behind other evidence of retribution, General Pollock evacuated Affghanistan, returning to India by Jellalabad. At Ferozepore "the illustrious garrison" was welcomed by Lord Ellenborough with every mark of distinction;—the Governor-General attributing to General Sale and his brave companions-in-arms "the salvation of the name and fame of the British empire in India."

"1843. *Army broken up. The 13th marches to Mobarukfore, and thence to the hill station of Kussowlee. Havelock resumes the religious instruction of his soldiers, which had also been kept up at Cabool and Jellalabad. His family returns from Eng-*

land. Goes with them on leave of absence to Simla. Is appointed to the rank of Major in his regiment, and nominated Persian interpreter to the new Commander-in-Chief, Sir Hugh Gough. Joins him at Cawnpore. Army of exercise assembles at Agra. Crosses the Chambul, and fights the battle of Maharajpore. On the conclusion of hostilities, the Commander-in-Chief tours through the State of Bhurtpoore, Deeg, &c., and reaches Umballa. At Delhi, news received of mutinous proceedings in several of the regiments. Commander-in-Chief proceeds to Simla."

He had scarcely sheathed his sword, and renewed his intercourse with his beloved family, when the trumpet sounded again, and he was summoned to the camp. An army, under the command of Sir Hugh Gough, had been organised to protect both the young Rajah of Gwalior, an ally of the British Government, and Scindia, whose recent fidelity to his treaty engagements thus far has won so much approbation.

On the 21st of December the Commander-in Chief, accompanied by the Governor-General, engaged the rebel troops at Maharajpore, while General Grey, at the head of a column of 8000 men, encountered an army of 12,000 at Punniar, in both cases with most successful results.

"1844. *Alarm of Sikh invasion. George Broadfoot appointed Governor-General's Agent in the North-Western frontier. Havelock promoted to the rank of Lieutenant-Colonel by Brevet. Lord Ellenborough recalled. The Commander-in-Chief, in expectation of a Sikh war, tours in the protected Sikh States and near the Jumna."*

He had by this time got detached from his old regiment, the 13th Light Infantry, with which he had been associated ever since he left England in 1823. Not more than five men were left of his original comrades. But religious services were as much in vogue as ever, and one of his last interviews with the regiment was one of which he spoke as an interview with "his little Christian flock."

During the past year horrid cruelties had been perpetrated in the Punjaub. Runjeet Singh, the old "Lion of Lahore," was dead, and the struggle for his throne had been the occasion for the successive assassinations of nearly all his descendants. Dhuleep Singh, then a mere child, had been placed upon the throne.

Deeming the security of the frontier a matter of vital importance to the safety of the North-West Provinces, Sir Henry Hardinge had for some months been concentrating a considerable force upon the line of road leading more immediately to the Punjaub, and when at length the Sikh soldiery invaded the British territory, he was not unprepared.

"Though much shrewd logic has been employed," writes Havelock, "and much lofty eloquence, to prove the reverse, the real fact appears to me to be that the rulers of India have generally, and not unreasonably, been dragged with unfeigned reluctance into the wars in which they have been engaged, and that the principle of nearly all those contests has, on the part of the British, been that of pure and unwilling self-defence."

"1845. *Return to Simla. George Broadfoot spends part of the season there. Sir Henry Hardinge repairs to the North-West Provinces. The Sikhs invade India. Battle of Moodkee, in which Havelock has two horses shot under him. Sir Robert Sale mortally wounded at Battle of Ferozeshuhur.*"

"21*st and* 22*d. George Broadfoot killed.*"

Up to the eleventh hour Sir Henry Hardinge entertained a sanguine hope that India might be spared a war with the Sikhs,—an opinion also entertained by Major Broadfoot. His hopes were disappointed. On the 13th December the Sikhs crossed the Sutlej, and on the same day war was declared. On the 18th the Governor-General and Commander-in-Chief reached Moodkee, and engaged the enemy, 12,000 strong, with twenty-two guns. After a protracted and obstinated resistance they were driven from their entrenchments with great loss. Waiting till the 21st for reinforcements, they again met the enemy at Ferozeshuhur with a force variously stated from 35,000 to 50,000 men, with nearly 100 guns. The action was prolonged with much obstinacy until darkness compelled the combatants to suspend the fight. The intervening night was one of intense anxiety to both commanders. Upon the issue of the battle, only yet begun, depended the name and, perhaps, the very existence of British rule in India.

"The night of the 21st December," wrote Sir Henry Hardinge, "was the most extraordinary of my life. I bivouacked with the men without food or covering, and our nights are bitter cold. A burning camp in our front, our brave fellows lying down under a heavy cannonade, which continued during the whole night, mixed with the wild cries of the Sikhs, an English hurrah, the tramp of men, and the groans of the dying. In this state, with a handful of men who had carried the batteries the night before, I remained till morning, taking very short intervals of rest, by lying down with different regiments in succession, to ascertain their temper and raise their spirits. . . . My answer to every man was, that we must fight it out, attack the enemy vigorously at daybreak, beat him honourably or die on the field. The gallant old General, kind-hearted and heroically brave, entirely concurred with me."

With daylight came a renewal of the fight. Placing themselves at the head of their columns, Sir Henry Hardinge and Sir Hugh Gough advanced. Keeping thirty yards in front, *to prevent the troops from firing*, they swept the enemy everywhere before them, capturing seventy-three pieces of cannon, and remaining masters of the field.

These actions had taken away two of Havelock's best and oldest friends—Sir Robert Sale and Major Broadfoot, the latter of whom had been lately his companion at Simla.

Could the conversations which he held with his friend during their pleasant intercourse at Simla be reported, it would be known that Havelock was as earnest with men of his own grade as with those below him on the subject of the fear of God. What were the highest earthly distinctions in comparison with those which were from above! He valued that approval which was due to honest and honourable men, and went all lengths with his companion in the appreciation of his Sovereign's or his country's praise. But, beyond all that, there was something better,—something, too, without which that would be good for little in the long run. And so, in their rides together, the friends thought of another kind of warfare than the one in which they were engaged professionally, and of the honour which cometh from the Lord only.

"1846. *Sikhs cross the Sutlej, and threaten Loodianah. Sir Harry Smith fights the battle of Aliwal. Battle of Sobraon. Havelock has a third horse smitten down by a cannon-shot, which passed through his saddle-cloth. Occupation of Lahore. Army breaks up. Commander-in-Chief returns to Simla. Havelock acts as Adjutant-General to Queen's troops. Is appointed Deputy-Adjutant-General to Queen's troops at Bombay. Proceeds to*

Calcutta to assume his appointment. Visits Serampore. Sees his wife's mother for the last time. The Sikhs defeated with great loss at Aliwal by Sir Harry Smith, and driven across the Sutlej."

There was now a brief lull in the campaign, although it was well known to both Generals that the enemy was strengthening his position at Sobraon. Considerable reinforcements arrived at the camp on the 8th, and the two commanders determined to move on this strong position, rendered all but impregnable under the direction of French and Spanish officers.

At daybreak on the 10th of February the action began. The Sikhs, who were 30,000 strong, maintained for hours a most determined resistance; nor was it until the entire division of infantry, with nearly every gun that could be sent to their aid, had been led to the attack of the batteries, that any impression was made. Gradually but surely, then, the bayonet cleared the way, and, after one of the most obstinate contests in the annals of India, victory was declared for the British.

The effect of this battle was decisive. Seeing that further resistance was hopeless, overtures were made to the Governor-General, but all consideration was rejected, until, with his army under the walls of Lahore, he dictated terms to the vanquished enemy, and occupied the capital of the Punjaub.

Having restored the youthful Maharajah Dhuleep Singh to the throne of "the Lion of Lahore," and leaving a garrison of 10,000 men, the two Generals, after a campaign of sixty days, returned to Simla.

The remarkable deliverance in the field, indicated in the above memoranda, led Havelock to render his warmest acknowledgments to his Almighty Deliverer. Three horses shot under him told plainly enough how near his wife and children had been to widowhood and orphanhood, and how narrow had been his own escape. It led to the repetition of the remark that he seemed to be specially protected amidst the greatest dangers. Though always amongst the foremost in the place of danger, he came off unhurt. And this continued to the end. His men and officers were ranked with the wounded and the slain in proportions far exceeding the casualties of Waterloo; but he went even through his last campaign untouched by sabre or ball, dying at last, when his end was come, not on the field of battle, but amidst the comparative quiet of his tent.

"1847. *Embarks with Sir George Clerk, the newly-appointed Governor of Bombay, in the 'Hindostan,' for Madras and Ceylon. Thence proceeded in the 'Auckland' steam frigate to Bombay. Receives intelligence of the death, at eighty, of Mrs Marshman. Health fails. Visits Mahbuleshur for recovery. Sir Willoughby Cotton succeeds Sir T. M'Mahon, as local Commander-in-Chief. Joins him at Poonah. Symptoms of liver complaint return. Tour in the Deccan, and return to Bombay.*"

Whilst at Poonah he wrote to his sister in England :—

"POONAH, *August* 21, 1847.

"MY VERY DEAR ——, ...

"Dear Hannah was restored to me almost by miracle. She is now, by God's mercy, convalescent, and her boy flourishes. My girls, too, are well. I also have improved in health in the Deccan, and eat, and drink, and sleep, and ride like a healthy man; but these appearances are fallacious. My health is perfectly shaken, if not wholly broken, by so many years of hard work in this climate. I ought to be off on the 1st of March for England. My circumstances hardly afford me any opportunity of doing so; but God has opened a way for me in thousands of difficulties, and He may do so in this. —Ever your affectionate brother,

"HENRY HAVELOCK."

No sooner did he settle at Bombay for a time than he identified himself actively with the friends of Christian truth there of every denomination. He assisted at all their meetings for the promotion of missionary and educational efforts; and communed at the Lord's Supper "with much pleasure, and he would humbly hope not without profit," with the Presbyterians of the Free Church of Scotland.

The failure of his health excited apprehensions of danger. His own belief was that he had incurred serious, if not fatal mischief on the day when he fought at Moodkee.

Towards evening he came to a well, and eagerly drank a full draught. His horse refused to taste the water, and very obviously recoiled. The horse was right, for the well had been poisoned by the Sikhs. From the effects of that draught his constitution never fully recovered.

"1848. *Recommended to return to England, but wishes to remain another year, if spared. Revisits Mahbuleshur. Returns to the Deccan. Colonel Brooke proceeds to join the army at Mooltan. Havelock appointed to act as Military Secretary to the Commander-in-Chief. Returns to Bombay. News of the fatal skirmish at Ramnugghur.*"

The "fatal skirmish" mentioned here was the one in which his elder brother, Colonel William Havelock, was killed, in the second Sikh war. This was the brother, it will be remembered, who obtained for him a commission in the 95th Rifle Brigade, in 1815. The following letter refers to the Colonel's death :—

"BOMBAY, 15*th Dec.* 1848.

"MY VERY DEAR SISTER,—I need not remind you how seldom I take up the pen to address you, though you were one of the greatest comforts of my youth and early manhood, and my heart still bounds at the recollection of those days. . . . The occasion of my writing is indeed mournful. In a cavalry action, fought on the 22d of November, our beloved brother William met a soldier's death at the head of his noble and cherished dragoons. . . . There our gallant brother fell, not until his regiment had sustained a heavy loss, and he had conquered the admiration and sympathy of every brave man that can look with delight on acts of a kindred spirit with his own. . . . His body has never been found, for no one has been able to approach the spot whilst the Sikhs yet remain in position. . . . To know that godliness with contentment is great gain will lighten this affliction to them, and cause it to work out in the end a more exceeding and eternal weight of glory. To how small a number our seven of a family —eight at first—is now reduced! As each falls in succession into the grave, is not the event a warning to those who remain to draw nearer and nearer to Jesus Christ? Then will He draw nearer to us, and be our stay here, and hereafter our everlasting portion.—Your affectionate brother,

"HENRY HAVELOCK."

"1849. *At the conclusion of the war, Havelock's regiment, the 53d, is ordered into the field. He proceeds by dâk through Indore to join it. Countermanded. Rejoins head-quarters at Mahbuleshur. Returns to the Deccan. Serious illness. Embarks for England, October 3d.*"

From Bombay he wrote:—

"BOMBAY, *April* 3, 1849.

"MY VERY DEAR ——,—I returned yesterday from a fruitless expedition in the direction of the Punjaub. My regiment, the 53d, having been ordered into the field, I obtained permission to proceed to join it. . . . . The expense of the trip proved to be great, and I made a great sacrifice of money in leaving my appointments here. But ever considering that duty is the first consideration, I did not hesitate. . . . . I had only reached half-way between Indore and Agra when a peremptory order reached me to retrace my steps to Bombay. . . . . It seems now determined that Hannah and my girls and little boy must embark for England on the 15th of this month. We have been so often disappointed, that I know not how to hope to see our wish realised. . . . . Still God is with us, and I will labour as long as I have life, and I will hope against hope as long as I can labour. Your news of Jos.'s change of heart is a cordial to my heart. God bless you.—Your affectionate brother,

"HENRY HAVELOCK."

Thus for these two-and-twenty years had he been walking with God in deed and in truth. And, through the preventing and sustaining grace that had been vouchsafed to him, he had been able to put to silence the ignorance of foolish men. His comrades, high and low, held him in respect. They knew that his religion was not put on for sinister or sanctimonious ends—that he was not pious at the prayer-meeting and profligate at the mess—that he walked worthy of his vocation at all hazards, and at any cost. Both in the general and the religious circle in which he moved he was alike esteemed. An excellent minister of the Free Church, who knew him intimately at Poonah and Bombay, bears the following testimony to his worth :—

"He was a man of a thoroughly Evangelical Alliance spirit. He was always happy to take part in meetings of the Evangelical Alliance, the Tract Society, Bible Society, the various Missionary Societies, and every work in which Christians of different churches came together.

"He attended meetings of a kind very common in India, for reading of the Scriptures, religious conversation, and prayer. In these meetings he evidently took a deep interest; but I do not remember his taking a prominent part either in expressing his opinion or asking questions.

"I need not say that he was greatly esteemed by members of all churches as a decided and consistent Christian, and that the presence of such men in India powerfully contributes to the advancement of the truth among the heathen no less than Europeans.

"When I lived in Poonah I had often the pleasure of meeting him in private. I found him, in addition to the sterling excellences of his religious character, a well-read, highly intelligent, animated, and, in all respects, most agreeable associate."

CHAPTER VI.

HAVELOCK'S VISIT TO ENGLAND.

TO the recommendations that he should leave India for a time, Havelock was at length constrained to yield. His health had become seriously impaired, and nothing less than entire cessation from his military duties would now avail for its restoration. His arrangements were made accordingly, and in 1849 he returned, after an absence of twenty-seven years, to his native land.

He reached England on the 6th of November. The first duty was to seek medical advice, and to ascertain what were the probabilities of recovery. He was encouraged by the opinions given about his case, and addressed himself hopefully to the course which he was directed to pursue.

Within a fortnight of his arrival he removed from London to Plymouth, taking with him his wife and children. There he resumed his intercourse with the sister to whom his letters had been sent from Poonah and Bombay. They were mutually happy, and found themselves almost at once deep in the reminiscences of the chequered past. They remembered how they were accustomed during his vacations to get away into remote and secluded parts of the Park at Ingress, where, far from observation, he would have a daily rehearsal of Napoleon's battles, taking up his positions, and marshalling his battalions under their several generals. They called to mind how, often, when disturbed as he was reading in the library, wrapped in what he called his "toga," he had rushed away to the wood, and clambered up a tree, book in hand, determined not to give to play the time which was allotted to his work. They recollected the 7th of January 1810, when their mother fell from her chair whilst he was reading to her from the Holy Scriptures, and they wept together as they recalled the scene of parting, when he was obliged to go back to school, and knew that he should never see his mother any more.

No change had the long seven-and-twenty years in India wrought upon her brother Henry in respect to his warm attachments to those he loved. His filial veneration was unabated, and his brotherly affection was flourishing in undiminished power. This the sister felt from the moment they met, and every day's observation and experience assured her that she was right.

One thing attracted especial notice. In younger life he had evinced a good deal of resentment at reflections which had been cast upon him because of his firmness in doing what he deemed right.

"As he began to feel the influence of God's Spirit on his heart, there was a manifest change. He became calm and patient under his heavy trial, and obtained such control over himself as to disarm his opposers. During the last happy years before he went to India, he was mild, gentle, and forbearing, and our meeting at Plymouth convinced me that no remnant of the irritability of his boyhood was left, but that to everybody and in everything he was kind, considerate, and Christian-like."

He soon found opportunities at Plymouth for doing good. Of visits to the sorrowing and the afflicted, grateful mention could be made. He knew exactly what portions of the Bible were suitable for the chamber of suffering, and went there prepared to speak a word in season to those who were weary. No commonplace or inappropriate or indiscriminate conversations did he introduce. Nor was he content with mere formal, semi-professional utterances. He sought out acceptable words, and ministered to those who were distressed the strong consolation of the everlasting gospel. His prayers, too, tended to the same kindly end. He had apprehended the unfailing sympathy of the Great Intercessor, and in the full assurance of faith had often found grace to help in time of need. Experience worked hope. To the mourner, in whose sorrows he was ever ready to sympathise, he said, Take courage. They might pray to God. And they knelt down and prayed, to the diminution of their griefs and to the conscious augmentation of their confidence in Him who comforteth those that are cast down.

In exercises of this kind his family were often reminded of a scene which occurred in 1835. He had been conducting a devotional service, in company with his household, amongst whom was an Irish servant-girl. She was melted to tears by the fervency and unction of his prayer, and, as she arose from her knees, addressed him with much emotion, "Oh, Misther dear, you 're not fit for a soldier. It 's too tinder-hearted you are. Sure, you was born a praist, and a praist it is you ought to be." The peculiarity was often recognised at Plymouth which this poor woman thus instinctively perceived—the unaffected earnestness and the remarkable aptitude which he evinced when drawing near to the throne of grace.

In January 1850, he left Plymouth for London, for a few days; and it is remembered by the friends by whom he was entertained that he never let a day pass without writing to his wife: she never failing to reciprocate the affectionate attention which was thus expressed. Most grateful are the recollections of that period to those who were especially his companions. There was a richness and depth of religious feeling which they were constrained to admire, and an appreciation of the religious privileges of his native land more intense than they could fully understand. To sit, or even to stand, in a crowded aisle, with multitudes all around him, listening to the glad tidings of great joy, was delightful to his soul; while, in the change respecting attendance on public worship which he noticed since he had left England, he found reason for thanking God and taking courage.

On the 6th of March 1850, he was presented at a levee at St James's by the Duke of Wellington; and next day he dined at Lord Hardinge's. On the 20th, he was present at a dinner given by the United Service Club to Lord Gough. On the 23d, when the East India Company fêted his Lordship, he was among the guests, recognising old comrades, and thoroughly enjoying this relaxation from military toil.

A painful duty awaited him on the 25th of March. The widow and family of his brother William, who had been killed at Ramnugghur, were expected at Southampton, on their return from India. It was felt by him incumbent to be there to receive them on the arrival of the vessel. Accordingly he went down, and shewed how able he was to bear the burdens of the depressed, and how ready he was to weep with them that weep. Well did he prove himself a brother to be trusted, and an uncle to be loved.

This duty fulfilled, he returned to Plymouth, and remained in the west of England till June; gradually recovering strength, and finding, day after day, opportunities for doing and getting good. Never, perhaps, was he happier than at this time. Circumstances around him were propitious, and companionships were congenial. In general society he was cordially welcomed, and by his Christian brethren he was increasingly esteemed. His family, too, was with him, and that always made his cup to run over.

About the middle of June he commenced a series of visits to several of his old friends and school-fellows—men of eminence and rank. To him, this renewal of intercourse was pleasant in the extreme; and he always referred to it afterwards as having been the occasion of great thankfulness to God. Opinions were canvassed, and differences of judgment were avowed and discussed. Substantial unity was ascertained in regard to the fundamentals of the Christian faith, and, in the assurance that the children of God would be all brought right at last, the old friends mutually rejoiced.

> "Absent in body, yet in soul they seem
> To hover near, and beckon back the hours,
> When from the sportive throng we sometimes stole
> To list the warnings of the great and good,
> And 'hold high converse' of eternal things.
> Hours of delight! and, if not all in vain,
> God's holy name be praised, and, with meek heart,
> His mercy sought to keep us to the end!"
>
> —*From a Poem by Sir W. N.,*
> *commemorative of this happy reunion.*

The intervening years since they parted had wrought upon the accomplished jurist, and the sound-hearted theologian, and the devout soldier, more or less of change in theologic creed and ecclesiastical practice, but no difference could they discover in that which constituted them men of God. Not a whit more conscientious was any one of them than were all the rest, and though they were by no means of the same mind about many matters of grave importance touching things to be believed and things to be done in the name of Christ their common Lord, yet they respected each other's consciences; resolving, not with any kind of formality at all, but at the dictate of a fraternal evangelical instinct, to walk by the same rule, and to mind the same thing up to the last point to which together they had attained.

It had been recommended to Colonel Havelock that he should take advantage of the medicinal waters of Germany during his stay in Europe. Having paid his visits to his early friends, he set out for Ems, as being one of the best places for prosecuting the object he had in view. His wife accompanied him, and the following letter will shew that the journey and the treatment to which he was subjected were advantageous to his health:—

"EMS, *Sept.* 10, 1850.

". . . We have had a pleasant and interesting journey to this place. At Dover we were detained by the very tempestuous state of the weather, and so we visited the barracks and parade in which I learnt a part of my military exercises in 1816. Then came a good night's tossing on the ocean. The rail carried us to Brussels, and the next day was devoted to Waterloo. Then a quiet Sabbath. Monday carried us to Cologne, and next day we reached by steamer Coblentz and Ehrenbreitstein. We have resided here nearly three weeks, and are all well pleased with the spot. At Coblentz I took counsel of Dr Soest, recommended to me by Sir W. Cotton, in 1847. . . . . I can hardly describe to you how much I have already benefited, by God's help, from these potations and immersions. . . . . I am to devour grapes at the rate of eight pounds per diem, and then it is hoped I may be fit for something. We shall see. Love to all."

. . . . . .

What with the grapes and the hydropathy together he rallied yet more sensibly, and became comparatively a vigorously healthy man.

It was now time to decide as to the course for the future. Anxious were the deliberations, and earnest the prayers of the parents, that God would direct them for the best. It was very soon decided that their daughters and little boy should be educated in Europe. With the knowledge that they had of India and of Indian society, they had resolved that those so dear to them should not receive their instruction or their introduction there. The desire to train up their children in the way they should go was paramount. To see them fearing God from their youth was the daily parental prayer. Intellectual discipline was a great object to be secured, with attainments and accomplishments befitting their condition; but moral and religious influences were desiderated at the same time, with a view to their personal dedication to the service of the Lord Christ. But there was a difficulty. There was no alternative for the father but to remain in India. No secret did he make of it that he could not relinquish his position there and return to live with his family, either in this country or on the Continent. Not so fortunate had he been as some others in obtaining patronage and its emoluments. Three-and-twenty years as a subaltern had not tended to make him a wealthy man. Provision for his wife and children beyond the time being had been altogether beyond his power. The course for himself he felt to be inevitable. To India he must return, leaving his children behind him.

The course, however, was by no means clear for Mrs Havelock. To accompany her husband was her first impulse, and upon doing this she was fully bent. He demurred on account of the children. They must not be committed wholly to the guardianship of strangers. What could be substituted for a mother's watchfulness and care? Who could do for the opening minds and the trusting hearts of their loved ones what she could do? So far as the father was concerned his mind was made up. He would go out alone. As best he could he would bear the pain of separation. It was not what he should sacrifice, it was what his little ones would gain. Had the attachments between them all been less affectionate or less active, it would have been a far easier task to determine what should be done. But they were so much members one of another, they were so knit together, and they were so mutually and tenderly endeared, that they were bitterly loath to part. Never, indeed, has the household tie been more sensibly or more obviously a fondly-cherished and indissoluble one, than in their case. By comparative strangers it was noticed almost immediately, and by those who knew them intimately it was more and more admired. On which side the affection preponderated it would have been impossible to pronounce.

Hence, to leave the children was a great trial, but to let the husband go out alone to India was a trial quite as great. The struggle was a sharp one, but in the end it was fixed that the children should have the benefit of their mother's guardianship, and that the father should return by himself. The time, however, would come when they should meet again. The education being obtained, mother and daughters would proceed to India, and altogether they would re-enjoy the domestic intercourse which was thus sorrowfully interrupted.

The decision once come to, with his usual promptitude Havelock arranged for carrying it into effect. It seemed to him that Bonn would be a suitable place on all accounts for the location of his family. Educationally and religiously it would supply the opportunities and appliances which were requisite, whilst it would be a residence of great pleasantness and healthiness for those whom he must leave behind. Accordingly he took a house at Bonn, which overlooked the Rhine, and there for six months he remained with his family, enjoying the neighbourhood and society greatly, and improving every day. Most assiduously and thoughtfully did he provide for the future comfort of its beloved inmates, so ordering everything about the dwelling that they have ever since been reminded of his fond solicitude for them in the prospect of his being far away. A pleasanter six months than that was never spent. The remembrance of it has been always grateful. It will be precious now for evermore.

During the month of September 1851, Havelock came to England to take leave of friends. He was in good health and most cheerful spirits, thankful for the blessings he had obtained by his relaxation, and assured that God would be his portion to the end.

Again he visited the house of mourning, and proved himself a bearer of the burdens of those who were in sorrow. "I would say," he remarked one day, "flee in your troubles to Jesus Christ. The experience of upwards of thirty years enables me to say, no man ever had so kind a friend as He, or so good a master. View Him not at a distance, but as a prop, a stay, and a comforter, ever at hand, and

He will requite your confidence by blessings illimitable."

A short time was spent in London and the neighbourhood, on his way from the West of England to Germany; and it was several times observed that he took his leave both of older and more recent associates with a tone of unfaltering confidence in the providence and grace of God.

This may be gathered from a communication to a friend, whom he was unable to visit for the purpose of saying farewell:—

". . . KENT, *October* 8, 1851.

"MY DEAR ——,—I write to bid you farewell, and to thank you very sincerely for all your very great kindness to me and my family since I came to London, after near thirty years' absence, in November 1849. On the 10th November I expect to be on board the steamer which is to carry me from Trieste to Alexandria, and on the 5th December I hope to land at the Apollo Bunder, Bombay. But all this is in God's hand. I have had in this land countless mercies to praise Him for, and though I leave it, not through desire to abandon it, but only from the conviction that the road to India is my path of duty, that very consideration emboldens me to hope for His protection and guidance by the way and during my sojourn, whether it may prove long or short."

Havelock left England, and stayed at Bonn until

the 27th of October, when it was his duty to set out for India. The morning arose upon him sadly. There were his loved ones as wakeful as himself at early dawn. Each felt what none could utter. Separation was now come—a sensible reality. Pleasant readings together were terminated. No more excursions would be planned and executed. Going to the house of God in company was past. *That refreshing and delightful family-worship* was all over; one more exercise, and the husband, the father, the master, would not be there officiating as the patriarch and the priest unto God. Even at the best of their choicest expectations, they should not kneel down together again for many, many years.

They knelt down then. Tremulous were the patriarch's tones; full, quite full, the heart of the priest of the weeping household, as he was making intercession for his wife and for their daughters and little son.

Who could tell the impending vicissitudes? Who could forecast the incidents of their separation? Who could prearrange for the emergencies in India, and for the possible and even probable necessities on the Rhine? He apprehended the uncertainty, but he staggered not at the promise of God through unbelief. God would watch between them whilst they were absent one from another. Asia and Europe were alike under the perpetual observation of their heavenly Father. They might at any moment regard it as the present fact that before they called the Lord would answer, and that whilst they were yet speaking He would hear. They had often said and sung together that removal from the Divine presence was impossible; that alienation from the love of God was inconceivable; that neglect of united and believing prayer offered at the throne of grace was as incredible as that the Holy One should lie. Now was the occasion for acting upon their long-cherished and devout convictions. They knelt, and arose with strength recovered. He in whom they trusted would never leave them nor forsake them. His grace was sufficient for them. His strength would be made perfect in weakness. Though their house in another hour would not be so with God, as they all lovingly desired, yet had the Lord made with them an everlasting covenant, ordered in all things and sure.

That memorable hour passed; the steamer arrived; the embarkation took place; the adieu, the last adieu of all, was stammered out; faces and forms vanished slowly in the distance, and Havelock was on his way to India—alone.

CHAPTER VII.

HAVELOCK'S DOMESTIC SOLITUDE.

SLOWLY the steamer moved up the Rhine, giving Havelock another opportunity of gazing on the different objects of his admiration, and of calling up to recollection the historical incidents with which his mind was so well stored. With each memorable place he was familiar, having at his command the ancient and modern narrations both of the great passages across the river and of the important events which had ensued. To the ruins of Roman encampments he could have pointed. Of the traditions of the mediæval castles he could have given an account. About the battle-fields of the last and present century he could have supplied accurate information, whilst with these military details he could have blended agreeable communications concerning the Moravian establishment at Neuwied. Fraught was his memory with the materials for intelligent enjoyment within himself, if unaccosted by the stranger; or for a traveller's, a scholar's, or a Christian's conversation, with those who were disposed to talk. He reached Coblentz in the afternoon, and went at once to the well-known Prussian fortress on the other side of the Rhine. But his affections were down the river. He could not suppress his sorrow. The separation weighed down his soul. He, the strong man, had no refuge but in God.

Amidst much "heart-wringing bitterness," the incidents of his journey were communicated day by day until his embarkation at Trieste :—

"COBLENTZ, *Oct.* 27, 1851.

"I got well up, by God's blessing, to this place, but not until four, and have since been up to, and over Ehrenbreitstein; but I will take no rest and no refreshment until I have written you a line. God bless you, Heaven's best earthly gift to me. Kiss for my darlings. H. H."

"FRANKFORT, *Oct.* 28.

"I arrived here this evening, and hope to get on to Leipsic to-morrow; but have really lost all desire to see anything or inquire about anything, for I have no one to whom I can communicate my feelings of pleasure or pain. I ought not to write thus, however, as it will grieve you. I have commenced this journey under God's guidance, and not an effort on my part shall be spared to do something for you and my little ones. If you knew what I have endured since I parted with you, I fear it would give you pain, but my God will support me. Remember, I am not the only one who sinks thus when separated from those dearest to him. Read the account of the great Marlborough under such circumstances. But I have Jesus Christ to trust to, and His presence to comfort me. Yet in this mortal state we do feel keenly. Pray for me. H. H."

"LEIPSIC, *Oct.* 30, 1851.

"I purpose going to see the battle-field of the Völker-schlacht, as the Germans call it, to-morrow morning, so I will commence another letter to you in the solitude of my chamber. Oh! how ardently I desired to turn back and rejoin you at Bonn, as I lay in my bed at Frankfort. It was a totally sleepless night, a thing, as you know, most unusual with me. I sat up meditating and writing until near eleven, and when called at six had not once closed my eyes; not even dozed or slumbered for a moment. The bitterness of parting, my position after so many years, which renders it unavoidable, and, I fear, not a few doubts about the worldly future, passed in rapid succession through my brain, which, without being in the least fevered, was so wrought upon that I never slept a single second. But I did indeed find sweet relief in the thought of meeting you in that better kingdom; for all earthly meetings are uncertain, and only terminate in longer or shorter separations. Join with me in prayer, that we, through faith in the blood of the Lamb, may be held worthy to partake in His resurrection, and be together with Him and our children in His glory. I know not what lies before me, but I *do* feel that we are both in the path of sacred duty. Let us do His will and leave the event to God. Perhaps He may be merciful to us, and grant that we may soon meet again, though we see not how. H. H."

"DRESDEN, *Oct.* 31, 1851.

"I have just got yours of the 29th. Thank God you are all well. To His gracious care I commend you all. You will find happiness among yourselves; but I feel for the present a sad houseless wanderer; but I must not repine, God is with me, that ought to be enough. To-day we have had snow all the day. . . . . The great delicacy here, and at Leipsig, are 'larks,' of which I have been partaking to-day, —not frolics (tell Georgy)—but real roasted larks! Kiss all *good* children for me. Ever, H. H."

"P.S.—My health is good, but the disease is in the mind."

"PRAGUE, *Nov.* 3.

"I stopped here chiefly if not entirely because I expected a letter from you, but have found none, and wish I had gone on towards Vienna, for I got in too late to see anything. To-morrow I purpose to run on at once to the Austrian capital. This morning, as I travelled up the bank of the Elbe, which runs between the pine-clothed hills of Bohemia, the heights were everywhere capped and fringed with snow and ice, and the margin of the river frozen.

I fell in at my hotel at Dresden with a Lieutenant Schomberg, a lineal descendant of the Duke who was killed at the battle of the Boyne, and a shrewd, active, sensible fellow, who had been to see all the fortresses in Austria, and on the Rhine, and knew a good deal about them. The Austrians searched my baggage this morning, but it was a mere form, excepting that the attention of the 'Visitor' was wonderfully attracted by the bulbs, and he dived through all the folds of brown, blue, and whited-brown paper to get at them. I laughed, and said they were for the garden in India, and then he stared and laughed too. He wanted also to know what was in my valise. I told him my Indian razzai and my sabres, and he looked comical, and said, 'Aha! a soldier—a colonel!' and declined further search. My passport has, however, been wanted all day long, and exchanged for all kinds of police papers and then given back again, and I should not wonder if a fellow comes for it in the middle of the night, the Austrians seem so fond of it."

"VIENNA, *Nov.* 5, 1851.

"Vienna is a very splendid capital in population and extent—the streets well built and clean—the public buildings stately, though generally without architectural beauty, and the environs highly picturesque. The churches are many of them magnificent, and the Cathedral of St Stephen's, the spire of which I ascended this morning, is far finer than

Cologne or Ulm. The presence of the mighty Danube give the city a noble air. The Belvedere Palace and its gardens are grand, though not highly tasteful. The gallery in it is filled with a very numerous collection, in strikingly good preservation, rich in two splendid Raphaels, two excellent Correggios, a masterpiece of Titian, and a perfect galaxy from the *studios* of Rubens, Vandyke, and the great Venetian's, one very fine Murillo, and numerous pictures of Jordaens and the Bolognese and Flemish schools. There is likewise a charming Pietro Perugino and a good Francia. But the collection is too numerous—that is, has too many second and third-rate pictures in it. But tell my girls I have now done with pictures, and begin to wish that I had left Europe without seeing any, for I fear such sights may unfit me for the stern duties which lie before me. Let them turn their hearts and minds to the great business of salvation, and learn to be practical persons, building their hopes of earthly satisfaction only on a sense of duty faithfully discharged, and their expectations of eternal blessedness on the merits of the Saviour. . . .

"Now—though the word tears my heartstrings—adieu! God may grant us a happy meeting sooner than we expect; but if never on earth, in the presence of Jesus I trust we shall meet."

His letters to his children have been seldom surpassed for the combination of the religious with the intellectual. He wrote to them invariably as a father anxious for their salvation; but at the same time he kept in view their different occupations and prospects in life, shewing them how they might use the world without abusing it.

"HOTEL DE FRANCE, DRESDEN,
Nov. 1, 1851.

"MY DEAR LITTLE H——,—I have this morning received, and thank you for, your good and sensible letter of the 30th October. It is pleasing to see the interest which you take in your studies, and, above all, in the lectures by which Mr G. strives to teach you the way of everlasting life. Your poor papa is in great pain of mind and heart just now, and does not fully enjoy anything, but he prays constantly for you and all his dear children, and fervently hopes to meet them in that better kingdom. As for the things of this world, they not only perish in the using, but are ever alloyed with extreme anxiety; but we must be thankful for all the blessings of our lot dispensed by a gracious God. I have had time only for two sights at this very nice place. I arrived late last evening, but this morning called on Herr L——, and went to the grand gallery. I think you would almost forget Munich if you were to see it. The building is, indeed, far inferior to the Pinakothek, but, though my survey was very hurried, I was enchanted with the pictures. I made my way at once to the *gems*. The Madonna di San Sisto, which an artist was copying, perhaps did not quite come up to the expectation raised by the prints. It is unspeakably fine, indeed, but sadly damaged by age, and has been cleaned and smeared by artists until much of its original splendour has departed. But on either side of it are two of the noblest Correggios I ever saw—far finer even than those in our National Gallery. Then there is La Belle Jardiniere, another Madonna of Raffaelle—beautiful! There are enough to make up a grand gallery; but the pictures are very numerous and excellent in all the schools. There are four churches, (which I saw,) two quite superb. Next, I mounted to the top of the Kreuzkirche, and thence saw, as on a plan, all that Napoleon saw at the grand battle, excepting the battle itself. He was there very often during the fight, and my guide saw him looking through his telescope, and writing rapid despatches and sending them off by his generals and staff, whilst his map and plans were spread on the roof of the tower. I do now understand Alison's account of the fight perfectly. I am quite well, tell dear mamma, and purpose to rest here to-morrow, the Sabbath, and then to proceed on Monday to Prague. May God's Spirit accompany me, and be ever with mamma, and you, and N., and little G., and the two dear boys in India.

"Your affectionate father,

"HENRY HAVELOCK."

On the eve of his embarkation, he wrote to his wife:—

"TRIESTE, *Nov.* 9, 1851.

"This morning I have got your dear letter, No. 8, of the 4th instant. I think I have not got more than seven in all, so one must have missed me—directed perhaps to Prague, perhaps to Dresden, perhaps to Vienna. . . . And now teach our girls and boy to serve God and honour the Lord Jesus Christ. Think of the joy of our all meeting again in that presence where there is no sorrow and no pain. If we meet again on earth, it will only be to part in heaviness, in heart-wringing bitterness, as we have lately parted; but, oh! that blessed meeting will know no separation. God be your portion in time and in eternity. Ever yours,

"H. H."

Colonel Havelock arrived at Bombay in December 1851. Correspondence at once commenced with his family on the Rhine, and continued, without intermission, mail by mail.

The incidents of his life in India come out in his letters to his children with great simplicity, and with invariable reference to the one thing needful. Incessant was his craving for home society at the earliest possible moment, and yet most earnest was his effort not to evince or to induce impatience against the will of God.

"MY DEAR GEORGE,—This is your birthday, and here I sit in sight of the house in which you were born, five years ago, to write you a letter. My office is gone down to Poonah, and I have nothing to do but think of you; but your brother J. is very busy in the next room, reading Mahratta with his pundit. However, he says that he too will scrawl a note for you as soon as his daily studies are over. I daresay H. is remembering you too; but he, you know, is a long way off from us now, in the Punjaub.

"Now, though a little boy, you ought to have wisdom enough, when you get these lines, to call to mind how very good God was to you on this day, in preserving the life of your dear mamma, who was so sick that no one thought she could recover. At that time, too, I was in very poor health; but am now so much better, by God's mercy, that I have not had any suffering to complain of since I returned to India; indeed, since I saw you last, when I got on board of my steamer at Bonn, to go up to Mainz, on my way to India. They tell me that now-a-days it is the fashion for little boys like you to do no work until they are seven years old. So, if you are spared, you have two more years of holiday; but then you must begin to labour in earnest. And I will tell you what you will have to learn: the first thing is to love God, and to understand His law, and obey it, and to believe in and love Jesus Christ, since He was sent into the world to do good to all people who will believe in Him. Then, as it is likely you will be brought up to be a soldier in India, you will have to be taught to ride very well, and a little Latin, and a great deal of mathematics, which are not very easy; and arithmetic, and English history, and French, and German, and Hindostanee, and drawing, and fortification. Now, you will say, this is a great deal—quite a burden, and a cart-load of learning. But if you are, from the first, very industrious, and never let any day but the Sabbath pass over without four hours' diligent study, at least, you will soon find that the mountain of learning before you is cut down into a very little hill indeed.

"Now, you must ask your mamma to read this letter to you, and explain to you all the words which you do not understand; and you must keep it, and read it over every birthday until you are twenty-one years old; and, year after year, you will be astonished at the little which you knew when you first received the letter, and how clearly you can comprehend that which then appeared difficult and strange to you. Moreover, you must on this day always read (that is as soon as you have learnt to read) the forty-sixth Psalm and the third chapter of the first epistle of John; and though at first, perhaps for some years, you may not comprehend much of them, yet, at the last, their meaning will be plain to you; and by the teaching of God's Holy Spirit, you will learn much good from them. Love always

"Your affectionate papa,

"HENRY HAVELOCK."

The father's anxiety for his sons was that they

might become good men. Greatness was not undesirable, but goodness was the one thing needful.

" . . . . . Do you, my little George, though you should be the lowest man in India, in rank and worldly endowments, take care that you have Jesus for your friend, and He will exalt you to share His glory in His kingdom. I am gratified by all that your mamma tells me of your conduct and application to your studies. But remember that this is a *fast* age. Every one is going at a tremendous gallop, so you must not move slowly, if you would, like your brothers, become an officer, and be a credit to your name and country. . . . . I have just returned from the tomb of the great man after whom you were named—Major George Broadfoot. He is called in the inscription on it, from the pen of his friend, Colin M'Kenzie, 'the foremost man in India;' and truly, in intellect and resolution, he was. . . . .

"Read all the accounts of the battles of Alma, Balaklava, and Inkermann; and if, by God's blessing, we meet again, I will explain them to you."

Havelock's practical wisdom in dealing with his children was remarkable. Aware how much depends in a religious education on the estimate which is formed of the Christian minister, he did his best to induce affectionate respect for the minister at Bonn on whose services his children attended. Let them hold the Rev. Mr Graham in reputation. It would gratify their father to learn that in his preaching and his friendship they continued to take delight.

TO HIS LITTLE GIRL.

"MY DEAR LITTLE N——,—I am almost an idle man to-day, so you shall at length have the benefit of my empty-handedness. I have been much pleased with all that you have written me since my return to India, and still more with the intelligence that your mamma has conveyed to me of your progress in your studies; and most of all with the account I have had of your attention to the lessons in Divine wisdom, given you by Mr G. You can never be sufficiently thankful for all the pains that good man has bestowed on you, nor half grateful enough to Almighty God for having put it into his heart thus to labour for the good of your soul, and the souls of others; and for having brought him to Bonn, as the scene of his Christian exertions. I pray daily that you may profit in heavenly things, and learn to regard Jesus Christ as personally your friend and benefactor; to come to Him for all that you need; to feel assured that all your sins are laid on Him; and that He will willingly and abundantly bestow on you, if you ask it diligently and in faith, the Holy Spirit, which He is commissioned to obtain for sinful human creatures. . . . . This place is charming, but how much more lovely must Germany now be, with its budding spring blossoms, its orchards, its lilacs, laburnums, and chestnut-trees! Be thankful for all its beauties, which no one would more delight to share than—Your affectionate papa,

"H. H."

Confidence in God for the future was strengthened by the recollections of the past. The Lord's former loving-kindnesses would be renewed to the parents and to their children after them.

"ESPLANADE, BOMBAY, *March* 13, 1853.

"I despatched you a pretty long letter yesterday, but on this Sabbath-day, which is also the day of your birth, I cannot refuse myself the satisfaction of writing a few lines to you. I trust the day finds you in health and peace,—the peace which the world can neither give nor take away, and which the knowledge of the glorious Gospel alone can impart. . . . It appears to me like a dream, so quickly have the twenty-four years passed away since we became man and wife. I may not—(who can say?)—live to see another of your birthdays, so now I will record how great have been your deservings, in upholding me in my many trials.

"But, above all, will be registered in heaven the care you have taken to train our five remaining children up for the blessings of eternity. . . . .

"May God guide you perpetually, and lead you into all holiness and truth.

"If I am spared to return to you, may our joint prayers obtain a blessing on those we love. On earth may you and I meet in peace, and in heaven in endless satisfaction." . . . . .

Before he left England he had seen the Crystal Palace, in Hyde Park. Reference had been made to the visit by a correspondent, who had told him that efforts were on foot to have the newly-projected palace at Sydenham made available for the public on the Lord's-day. His opinion was decisive :—

"BOMBAY, *Feb.* 9, 1853.

"MY DEAR ——, . . . True it is, as you remark, that family separations, such as you advert to, are ever painful; but the safest of all paths is the path of duty,—and it seems to be allotted to me to labour here until the end of my days; and whilst I remain here I cannot deprive my girls of a mother's care, nor dream of bringing Master George to this rather fervid island.

. . . . . .

"I did see your Crystal Palace when I was in England, though hastily. . . .

"No, you must have no Crystal Palace open on the Sabbath, if you value the small amount of piety to be found in the nation.

"Here we have many godly men, whose society is a comfort, besides a bishop, who is sincere and holy;

and many among the Presbyterians, who are most worthy."

Havelock was mindful of memorable days, both in his domestic and his professional life: finding in their annual recurrence the occasion for stirring up his own mind by way of remembrance, and for instructing and encouraging those he so much loved.

"MAHABLESHWUR, *April* 5, 1853.

". . . Whatever, in God's good providence, has betided or shall betide, I will write you a few lines on the day on which I have completed my fifty-eighth birthday. . . . . Here I am, in the same house which I inhabited last year. I could get no other. Every corner of it reminds me of Harry and Jos., who are not here. But I am deeply thankful for all the good which God has vouchsafed to both of them." . . . .

"*April* 7.

"This is my Jellalabad anniversary. It was rich mercy that preserved me on that day. The same goodness has watched over me in the eleven years intervening. . . . . Tell George that he must learn to ride. H. and N. should emulate their good brothers in diligence in worldly things, and labour, too, for the meat which perisheth not."

It was the wish of this most devoted father that

his children should attain to the greatest accuracy in every kind of knowledge. Accomplished himself, he wished them to become so, and to give proof of it even in minuter things. Let Georgy's name be spelt correctly, as no doubt it was in all future letters after the following lesson in English and Scotch abbreviations:—

"MAHABLESHWUR, *April* 28, 1853.

"This is our express day, so I have pitched the clerks and business out of the windows, and begin on little H.'s letter. [A little remark to her.] The English abbreviation of George is Georgy, not Georgie, which last is decidedly Scotch. People have yielded to this mode of spelling since the great Sir Walter set the fashion, but it is wrong. Thus write Charly or Charley, not Charlie, though it so appears in Scotch Jacobite songs.

"I am in the midst of 'Uncle Tom,' and—shall I confess it?—twice shed tears over it last night. I read on, and looking suddenly at my watch, found it was midnight. I must be very old, for I have shed tears of joy again this morning over little H.'s good letter! H. H."

"POONAH, *July* 2, 1853.

"Cassidy has preached a very eloquent sermon this morning to the Presbyterian congregation (chiefly 78th Highlanders) in the Assembly Rooms.

". . . The pictures of our three eldest children,

and of the cottage at Simla, are great companions to me. Yet I keep always wishing you had them in Germany. They would complete your little fire-side, or *stove*-side, comforts there. Whereas I have nothing to do but to scramble on here through as much of my six years as God allows me; for I will not stay longer, if spared, without another taste of European air!

"A son of Dr Knox, who went with me to Ava in 1826, has just been to call. As I spoke to him of his father, he said, drawing a ring from his finger, 'Perhaps you will recognise this.' It was the exact counterpart of that ruby ring which the Burman monarch gave me; the ring, you know, perished, with other valuables, in the flames at Landour, together with my golden patent of Burman nobility. H. H."

In the mission on which he went to the King of Ava in 1826, Havelock had been formally invested with a title of nobility and an official dress. These were the things destroyed in this fire.

"MAHABLESHWUR, *June* 4, 1853.

"MY DEAR GEORGE,—To-morrow is the Sabbath, and also your birthday. If spared until to-morrow you will be six years old; so in sight of the house in which you were born, I am again permitted to write to you, and wish you many happy and holy returns of the day.

"I trust your dear mamma will deliver this letter to you, and explain it all, where it needs explanation; and I wish you to keep it for a few years at least, that you may remember that you have a papa who, though distant from you for the present, and likely to be long distant, under no circumstances of time or place forgot you, but was constantly asking of God to bless you, and to send you His Holy Spirit to lead you into all truth and all good

"Things are much changed, George, since I was a boy. In the month of January 1800, (this is 1853,) my brother William and I were taken on ponies away to school at Dartford, three miles from Ingress, where we lived, (you have been in the county of Kent,) and set down at once to our learning. I was not five years old until the April after. Now you seem to have had a long holiday; no schooling yet, though you are six! But I trust you have learnt a little from your dear mamma's instruction, and that you are willing to learn a great deal more. Now, we can none of us tell what shall befall us, since God orders all, and will not tell us beforehand what shall happen; but it is likely that all my sons must earn their bread as soldiers. So very early I wish you to learn to ride, as one of the things most necessary for a soldier. I hope, before you are seven years old, you will have made some progress in this branch of learning. Your uncle William rode very well before he was seven. Now I must say farewell, dear George.—Ever your affectionate father, HENRY HAVELOCK."

"POONA, *Sept.* 8, 1853.

"MY DEAR LITTLE H——,—Your valued letter of the 17th July, which duly reached me, now demands a reply. I was much gratified by your account of your trip to England, which appears to have been full of interest and enjoyment. My last from your dear mother, brought you all as far as Lucerne, in your second Swiss journey; and I anxiously expect further details of your travels in the land of lakes and mountains. But my opportunities of writing are just now a good deal circumscribed, and time is short, and eternity at hand; so I must not delay to speak to you on the most important of all subjects—the care and prospects of your immortal soul. You have reached the age when your character ought to become fixed. Do not suffer yourself to be deceived by the false names which men give to things; but look steadily at the abiding truth, that mankind are divided into two classes—the children of God, and the servants of the world and its prince Satan. Make at once your choice for that good part which shall not hereafter be taken from you. Come to the Lord Jesus Christ, and ask Him for instruction and enlightenment of mind, and change of heart; and then do all that He commands you, and you shall be happy for ever. I cannot, at my age, expect to be long spared to labour for you. So, ponder my words.—On earth, or in Christ's better kingdom, I shall be ever your affectionate father,

"HENRY HAVELOCK."

Greatly was he gladdened by news from Mrs Havelock, of her having derived advantage from a tour in Switzerland.

"*October* 10, 1853.

"The express came in on the 5th, bringing your letters announcing your safe return to Bonn, after visiting Montanvert, Chamounix, and the Mer-de-Glace. I have not been at any of these; I only saw the summit of Mont Blanc from the neighbourhood of Geneva. I praise Almighty God for His great mercies to you on your journey; and it is matter of much satisfaction to me that you have made so safe and pleasant an excursion."

In his MS. Memoranda, we find that the time of his being thus near Geneva was 1823. In a journey amidst the mountains Havelock nearly lost his life. The horses of the carriage in which he was travelling became restive, and the harness giving way, "the whole equipage was within half a minute of being overturned into the abyss below."

"POONA, *Dec.* 11, 1853.

"You remind me that we have been two years

separated; and yesterday I completed my second year of my second term in India. But duty forbids any thought of striving to abridge the term of our separation. You must labour in the instruction of the dear children at home, and I for their good here as long as God shall ordain it, and give me health and strength to carry it out. But, most truly, you remark, that our mercies, during the period which has elapsed since I left you on the Rhine, have been unspeakable. The improvement in your health, and the health and progress of the younger three, my being sustained in my labours here, the spiritual instruction the children receive at Bonn, and our both being spared to see so much of friends long at a distance from us—are a few, amongst those numerous, I should say numberless blessings."

"BOMBAY, *Jan.* 11, 1854.

"You may conceive, better than I can describe, how much I was distressed and alarmed by the sad account of influenza having attacked you all, but especially you—dearest of all—with such violence. My apprehensions were the more vivid, because I know you never yield unless really and seriously ill. However, I build on the hope that the worst was truly over when you wrote, and that your next will announce the recovery of the whole party. It would be base and ungrateful in me to murmur, since almost every letter that I have received, from the day of my leaving you on the Rhine, has told me only of health and welfare. This trial of sickness is, doubtless, sent us for good—may we so improve it. At such moments we more fully feel that it is a happy thing, beyond description, to have a heavenly Father and a powerful Friend in whom to put our trust. In that better kingdom, which He has promised to His people, we shall have minds not to be assailed by sorrow, and bodies that sickness and decay cannot touch. H. H."

"*May* 9, 1854.

"We know not what an *hour* may bring forth. Since I finished my letter the mail came, announcing that I am Quartermaster-General. Let us thank God for this apparent mercy, and beseech Him to bless it, and make it a mercy indeed.

"If my life be spared so long, I shall return to Europe in three years. H. H."

"MAHABLESHWUR, *May* 16, 1854.

"This moment the characteristic casket has arrived; and though it has found me in the midst of employment, and overwhelming and distracting botherations about my expected move, I have opened it,—and there is the portrait. I never saw a more striking perfect likeness. The painter, German-like, has given you a sterner air than becomes an Englishwoman, but it is a most exact, faithful, living likeness; and with its Drachenfels in the distance, well painted. It seems as if sent to soothe me when I was fevered with cares. C——, the missionary, his wife, and remaining child, leave the hills the day after to-morrow for England. We had a meeting for prayer on occasion of his departure. I think about twenty-five or thirty really pious persons were present. This was a church. . . . I purpose to write again from Bombay before I leave. H. H."

The society of his two sons had served greatly to solace Havelock's solitude. To be parted from them was a sore trial, whether from the eldest at another time, or from the second now.

"BOMBAY, *May* 30, 1854.

"The day after to-morrow I purpose, God willing, to embark for Point de Galle, *en route* to Calcutta. Yesterday I took my leave of J. I put him on board his boat, and he and I parted with 'words and thoughts,' as Wordsworth wrote, 'too deep for tears.' God bless him! If I were a beggar on a dunghill it ought to be riches to me to have such a son. He is pious without an ounce of affectation, a genuine child of God's own sonship. He has very good abilities, good health, good habits. He is laborious, modest, self-denying, conscientious to the last scruple. Dear fellow, he loves you all with the sincerest love, and I came back to my club, feeling that I had parted with a treasure. God is with him.

"H. H."

"SIMLA, *July* 9, 1854.

"Yesterday, after sixteen days' incessant travelling, I reached this place in good health, though a little fagged, for which God's name be praised. . . . At Serampore I rose early in the morning and visited the printing-office, the manufactory, the college, all venerated scenes. In the chapel I saw the monumental slab to your dear mother's memory, on the same wall with those of Carey, Ward, Marshman, and Mack. The next building was empty. I read two chapters in the Bible on the table before the pulpit, and prayed alone. H. H."

"COMMANDER-IN-CHIEF'S CAMP, PESHAWUR,
Dec. 18, 1854.

"This morning we came into this well-known city. . . . I have waited until the latest safe day for the news that might arrive by telegraph from the seat of war. My patience is rewarded by the intelligence of the glorious but sanguinary action of the 5th November in front of Sebastopol. I wish my boy George to be fully instructed regarding these matters, for now that I am nearly sixty I derive great advantage from the knowledge I acquired at school of the affairs of those times."

"GOOJERAT, *Jan.* 15, 1855.

"In the *Gazette* of December 8 I find I am Adjutant-General to Her Majesty's Forces; so now I must prepare for hard work again."

"COMMANDER-IN-CHIEF'S CAMP, *Jan.* 31.

"I commence my duties as Adjutant-General on arrival at Ferozepore at the end of the present week. How my health will stand the work I cannot, of course, predict; but I trust I shall not be left without God's grace to guide me right. H. H."

The following reference to his old schoolfellow, Archdeacon Hare, will be perused with interest. On many points of great theological importance the two men were wide asunder; but they were one in Christ. Had Havelock been reading "Hare's Mission of the Comforter," he would not infrequently have protested. Much more frequently, however, he would have devoutly acquiesced. His friend, the Churchman, was a true-hearted servant of their common Lord.

"SIMLA, *March* 26, 1855.

"Yesterday I got two letters from Norris, in which he gives me full particulars of the last illness, death, and funeral of our friend Julius Charles Hare. He had the root of the matter in him, and is now with the Redeemer. Norris reminds me, that of the five who crept up into the sleeping-rooms in our school-days to read a sermon, two are now in the grave, and, I would add, the remaining three sexagenarians, or thereabout. May our short time be spent to God's glory!"

"*April* 5.

"I have risen this morning, and find myself sixty years of age. God's mercies have been unspeakable!"

The reminiscences of his marriage life were always grateful. The combination of the humorous with the serious in his twenty-sixth connubial salutation of "The best of mothers," marks significantly the high estimate of his obligations to God on her account.

"HEAD QUARTERS' CAMP, GUGRAON,
Feb. 9, 1855.

"Notwithstanding the reproach under which I live of being non-observant of notable days, I have not forgotten that, twenty-six years ago, not having been able to muster moral courage enough to run away against the tide in an Indian canoe, I consented to give 'hostages to fortune,' and braved the worse dangers and difficulties of domestic life. I have not repented, that I will seriously assert and maintain. On the contrary, my submission to the 'yoke' has been the source of nearly all the satisfaction and happiness which retrospect presents to me on the chequered map of my sixty years' existence. So, madam, all hail! best of mothers, and not worst of wives, accept my congratulations, and give me credit for the sincerity and the warmth of the affection which urges me this day to pray for your temporal and eternal blessedness, and points to you as the foundation of my own best recollections and hopes."

"SIMLA, *June* 22, 1855.

"I have often intended to mention regarding the passage in one of the prophets which is apparently becoming a family tradition, that it was not on the morning of the 7th April (Jellalabad-day) 1842 that I read Jeremiah xxxix. 16–18,—'Go and speak to Ebed-melech the Ethiopian, saying, Thus saith the Lord of hosts, the God of Israel; Behold, I will bring my words upon this city for evil, and not for good; and they shall be accomplished in that day before thee. But I will deliver thee in that day, saith the Lord: and thou shalt not be given into the hand of the men of whom thou art afraid. For I will surely deliver thee, and thou shalt not fall by the sword, but thy life shall be for a prey unto thee: because thou hast put thy trust in me, saith the Lord,'—which would have been very inappropriate to the circumstances, but on or about the 19th October 1841, when I was pondering on certain vague intimations I had received from the Affghans of the coming storm, in the shape of an awful insurrection then concocting.

"I had assisted at the forcing of the Khoord Cabul Pass on the 12th, and brought back the despatch to General Elphinstone, and was debating in my own mind whether it was my duty to remain with him, or to offer my services again to join Sale and assist him in his operations. Cabool was at that time, on the surface, in perfect tranquillity. Read over the verses in the light of this explanation, and you will feel their force, and how they were fulfilled to me.

H. H."

"SIMLA, *Jan.* 1, 1856.

"Here is the first day of another year! I praise God for all His mercies of the year 1855, and trust that His grace will be given me to live or die to His glory in that which is now beginning. The weather up here is splendid. No snow yet. The hill men are coming up in hundreds to carry down our things. We are to remain at Umballa until we hear of the arrival of the new Commander-in-Chief, General Anson, in Calcutta, and then proceed to the commercial capital. God bless you all!

"H. H."

"KURNAL, *Jan.* 19, 1856.

"Your dear letters, just received, have removed a mountain of anxiety off my mind. I praise God that you are restored to health again, and have once more reached your pretty domicile under the shadow of the Drachenfels.

"I am forcibly reminded, by my arrival at this place this morning, of my reaching it just twenty years ago—adjutant, not adjutant-general; seeing the truth in the glass of the Scriptures, and upholding it by every effort in my power. May my dear girls (one of whose birthplace this is) walk, as their mother and grandmother walked before them, and with more abundant grace, unto the end!

"H. H."

"DELHI, *Jan.* 28, 1856.

"Do not you wish you were here, purchasing shawls and jewels? General A. has arrived in Calcutta, and I am off to join him immediately. God bless you! H. H."

"CALCUTTA, *May* 6, 1856.

"I wish to draw your attention particularly to 'the boy's' military education. The Germans are good mathematicians; but every nation has its own peculiarities, and an English officer would, I suspect, after all, be best trained in England. I wish this boy to have advantages I never possessed, in a really good military education. And let his riding be well attended to.—Ever, H. H."

On one occasion Havelock thus described the peculiarities of the German soldiers:—"They seem to shine only as outpost cavalry. There their cat-like caution, patient watchfulness, talent for purveying for man and beast, and love of the animal that does half the work, tell admirably. One would fancy, too, that the German hussar caught spirit and intelligence from his horse." The next letter is full of sentiment and incident:—

"CALCUTTA, *Sept.* 17, 1856.

"Your letter of the 7th August, written in your own beloved, though yet weak hand, reached me last night; and I praise Almighty God, the Father of us all, and of the Lord Jesus Christ, that you are restored to me once more, as it were, from the grave, and I trust in His mercy to give you complete recovery. . . . I write in all the whirl of preparation. We are off by steam on the 22d, for the Upper Provinces. . . . The good old missionary, Fink, was called suddenly to his rest a week ago. I used to shake hands with him every Sunday on the steps of the chapel, in the Circular Road. On Monday I received notice to attend his funeral. He had been found dead on his sofa the day before, having lain down to sleep, apparently well. . . .

"I am touched to the heart by your favourable account of the dear girls; and, regarding the mighty George, as in other matters, you have done all things well. H. H."

"FLAT MATABAUGAH, NEAR CUTWA,
Sept. 27, 1856.

"Since the 22d we have been slowly steaming this sacred stream, or rather buffeting the waves of this inland sea, the banks of which you and I so well knew in the days of our humility. I pointed out, as we passed, every well known spot in Serampore to Seymour; walked over every foot of Chinsurah with General Anson and suite, and we coaled this morning at the ghat of William Carey, the missionary. You will remember our visit of 1834. The same God protects us now. . . . May God, if it be His pleasure, grant us once more on earth a happy meeting; if not, in heaven may we meet and be for ever re-united! H. H."

About this time a brother-officer met with an accident which ended in his death. There was danger that the income on which his widow must rely would lapse. With characteristic kindness and promptitude, Havelock interfered, and the source of income was saved. No letter, however, records this act of friendship. It has been communicated since his death.

"On the Ganges below Patna,
Oct. 13, 1856.

"I can, under present circumstances, only hope to keep up a regular communication with you by writing when opportunity offers. Here we are in well-remembered districts, for I passed the children's little dog's grave at Bhar this morning, where we coaled, and have, since the 22d September, been toiling up against stream with weak steam, past the shores which we skirted in company in 1831, 1833, 1840, and 1846.

"Your letters of the 23d August reached me at Berhampore, after I had despatched my letter from that place. There, and at Moorshedabad, we were hospitably entreated by M., whom you will remember as a Jellalabad hero. He is guardian of the Nawab Nazim . . .

"Am cut to the heart by the poor account you still give of your health; but trust your projected trip in Switzerland will, by God's blessing, give you strength again, and that you will many years be enabled in His good providence to watch over our two dear girls, and the mighty George's education. . . . God knows how my heart yearns to see you all again. But my duty is here, and I have several difficulties. If by God's aid I surmount them all, I shall, at the end of my three years' labour and self-denial, feel entitled to look upon you again. God grant it may be in health, tranquillity, and competency! . . . If it be God's pleasure, may you and I have one more happy meeting on earth; if not, a far happier in heaven! H. H."

"ON THE GANGES, OFF GHAZEEPORE,
Oct. 31, 1856.

"You will learn that Lord Hardinge died at South Park on the 24th of September,—I think very nearly five years after my taking leave of him at the porch of his mansion, when he remarked, that if I was going to India for five years, it was not likely that I should see him again on my return. . . . I am deeply grieved by your account of the illness of my dear boy, the mighty George. I trust the tour will do him good. Though separated, we can unite ever in prayer for our dear children."

The epithet "mighty" had been applied to George in pleasantry before his father's departure from Europe, and was now in the same pleasantry frequently employed.

"STEAMER ON THE GANGES, BELOW CHUNAR,
Nov. 5, 1856.

"At Benares I got yours of the 20th of September from the Schweizer Hof Lucerne, and wished very much I had been at the latter place also. I hold to my purpose as strongly as ever, I trust, of drawing on the Bank of Faith, but have learnt in my old age that there is another establishment, too much before neglected, to which God's Spirit as strongly invites attention—viz., the Bank of Prudence. . . .

"I praise God for your improved health and George's convalescence."

"LUCKNOW, *Nov.* 25, 1856.

"The day before yesterday I got your cherished letter of the 8th of October, bringing you back again to Bonn. I praise God that your little journey has given you, under His blessing, increased health and strength. In the midst of our hurry and bustle here, Mr J. Bensley Thornhill, who is to be married to my niece, Mary Havelock, has come to make my acquaintance. He is gentleman-like, clever, a good public servant, of sound intellect, and will, I should think, make a good husband."

It had been arranged that some time during

the year 1857, Mrs Havelock and one or two of her children should rejoin the General at Bombay. Great was the delight on all sides. Letters were full of congratulations. Not a happier family could have been found on earth. All the home-born household sympathies were in congenial action.

Just as the expectation was at its highest, letters arrived from him, lamenting that disappointment had become inevitable, through the declaration of war against Persia. "The sudden call of duty" was imperative. The command to which he had been appointed must be undertaken. His wife and daughters were not more grieved at the event than he was, but he had no alternative, and they must mutually forego their meeting until more peaceful times.

"Begumabad, on March from Meerut towards Delhi,
Dec. 13, 1856.

"You have done your duty nobly to your children, as ever, so especially since I left you for India in October 1851. This I fully acknowledge on earth, and God's righteous verdict will corroborate it in heaven. But you must postpone all plans of coming out to India. . . .

"Mary Havelock was married by the Bishop of Madras, on the 6th inst., to Mr John Bensley Thornhill."

"Agra, *Jan.* 6, 1857.

"Lord Elphinstone has telegraphed General

Anson, offering me, at Sir James Outram's recommendation, a divisional command in the Persian expedition. I have accepted, and expect to start immediately for Bombay. At my time of life the undertaking is arduous, but I go in faith in Him who has led me so long and guided me."

Everything within his power did he attempt in order to reconcile his family to this unexpected trial. To the promises of the gospel he referred them, and with the considerations of life and immortality did he seek to comfort their hearts and his own.

It was not joyous to any of them, but grievous. Nevertheless, it might afterwards yield the peaceable fruits of righteousness.

CHAPTER VIII.

HAVELOCK IN PERSIA.

WE were now at war with Persia. Russian diplomacy had succeeded in placing that country in an attitude of hostility to Britain, rendering the continuance of amicable relations with the Court of Teheran impossible. On the 1st of November war was declared, and on the 19th of January the first part of the expedition from India put to sea. Of the share Havelock took in the military transactions of that period the best idea will be formed from his own letters. He had written last from Agra, where his appointment to a divisional command had reached him. He was now at Bombay.

"PARELL, BOMBAY. *Jan.* 23, 1857.

"I have, by God's rich mercy, got through my long and rather trying journey from Agra. I here found H. established with the kind Governor, who has befriended him in every way, and has located me too, with every hospitable attention, in his well-known mansion.

"I am nominated in orders to command the Second

Division of the army employed against Persia, having two Brigadiers under me. H. is employed at the head-quarters of the force, in the Q.M.G.'s department. Lieutenant-General Sir James Outram commands the whole force. To his and Lord Elphinstone's good opinion I owe my nomination. The command is responsible, but my trust is in God. It is a rare thing for an officer in the Bengal Presidency to be summoned to command Bombay troops. I never should have solicited such a command, and would in truth rather have been employed in the North-west Provinces, where it is not unlikely that a force may hereafter be employed. But when the post of honour and danger was offered me by telegraph, old as I am, I did not hesitate a moment. The wires carried back my unconditional and immediate acceptance. . . . How many kind old faces have I recognised here! and all give me a hearty welcome."

The children of this happy family were as mindful as their parents of the domestic anniversaries in which they so much rejoiced.

"STEAMER PUNJAUB, BASSADORE,
Feb. 9, 1857.

"H. reminded me early this morning of this auspicious day, and I cannot refuse myself the satisfaction of writing you a few lines upon it. God may yet grant us some returns of this our twenty-eighth wedding morn, and may in His goodness only cause this increased separation to tend to our more speedy meeting. At all events, we are both under His eye in the path of duty.

"I embarked on the night of the 26th, but did not get clear of the harbour until the 29th, meanwhile resisting more than one invitation of the Governor to come back again to my good quarters at Parell. On the morning of the 27th the battery on the Apollo Bunder fired a salute, as I was supposed then to have gone on board—the first expense of the kind to which I have ever put the Indian Government. We have had some rough weather, but many mercies; and, after coaling at this wild place, hope to be at Bushire about the 13th or 14th.

"It seems probable that a part of the force will sail up to the mouths of the Tigris and Euphrates, and then ascending the little river Karoon, endeavour to seize the town of Schuster, and thence organise and advance towards Teheran. You will find the stream and the towns on the small German map of Eren, by Carl Kitter. It also exhibits the island of Kishur, and Bassadore, our present place of sojourn, and Bushire, whither we are proceeding. I know not at present whether it will be my lot to march to Schuster or defend Bushire; in fact, all is conjecture until we reach that port, and receive orders from our friend, Sir J. Outram. I only hope I shall be strengthened to do my duty, whatever task is assigned to me."

Of the justice and generosity of his country, should he fall in its service, he had no doubt. The Sovereign in her personal sympathy with the people's will, would take care of his wife and children. Had he known, at the time, how spontaneously and liberally this would ultimately be done, he could not have written more confidently..

"BUSHIRE, PERSIA, *Feb.* 18, 1857.

"H. and I are, thank God, well. Our operations will soon extend to Mohammerah, a place below the junction of the Tigris and the Euphrates. Our expedition against this point will sail in a few days; but steamers will carry letters from it to the Presidency. Pray that I may faithfully discharge to the end every duty. I have good troops and cannon under my command, but my trust is in the Lord Jesus, my tried and merciful Friend, to Him all power is entrusted in heaven and on earth. Him daily seek for me, as I seek Him without shadow of doubting. . . . If I fall in the discharge of my duty, the Sovereign will provide for your wants. . . . I am most happy in being under the orders of Sir James Outram, who is as kind as he is brave, skilful, and enterprising. Give my love and H.'s love to H., N., and George."

"CAMP, BUSHIRE, *March* 1, 1857.

"A sailing vessel leaves to-morrow, and I lose no

opportunity of writing, though I have little to communicate. Our expedition to the mouth of the Euphrates is delayed by adverse winds, which keep back our reinforcements; by the difficulty of embarking our troops and stores in an exposed and shallow roadstead; and the poverty of our steam means. Meanwhile, we have abundant causes of thankfulness; we and our troops are abundantly supplied with every kind of provision; the regiments are healthy, and the climate cold and bracing. An encampment on a sandy plain, surrounded with entrenchments, in front of a small Asiatic town, with its gray stone curtains and round towers, and a horizon of sea and date trees is not very lively; but soldiers have soldiers' resources.

"I am occupied in looking after my troops, and pondering on the events which cannot be far distant. Sir James Outram is all kindness and good fellowship, and there are some estimable men in our camp. H. H."

"CAMP, BUSHIRE, *March* 7, 1857.

"It is great cause of thankfulness to me that yours, commenced on the 31st December 1856, and continued on the 7th January 1857, has safely reached me,—for communications up this Gulf are, of course, not quite so regular or so safe as between Kensington and Hammersmith. Your letter came in by steamer yesterday, and I was gratified by the affectionate remembrance of me by all at Bonn at the end of the old and beginning of the new year."

"CAMP, MOHAMMERAH, *March* 28, 1857.

"Our expedition against this place has been entirely successful, but the victory was won by the Indian navy; the troops of my division, which landed in the best order and in the highest spirits, had not a shot to fire. The Persians were commanded by a Shahzada, and their works were formidable, but in three hours and a half they were so hammered by our war-ships, that the enemy abandoned them in dismay, suffering great loss; and before my regiments and cannon could be landed in the date groves, intersected by water-courses, and my columns formed, they were in full retreat, followed by a handful of cavalry. I had not a single casualty in my crowded troop-ship, and in the *Scindian*, in which H. was embarked, the only man killed was his head servant, who was smashed by a cannon-ball that had traversed the vessel from stem to stern, where the poor man met his fate. I had hoped that my troops would have won laurels, but Providence decreed it otherwise. We must be ever thankful for the preserving mercies of the day, the 26th of March. The cannonade was warm, and my steamer, the *Berenice*, crowded with Highlanders, led the troop-ships to the point where we landed. I felt throughout that the Lord Jesus was at my side. I am on shore here, without money, clothes, and almost without food or drink, but every want has been supplied.

"H. and I have a captured Persian tent over us, and we are as *jolly* as the two parsons you and I met in the railway carriage. The work inspires and animates me, and God is with me. I never felt better, God be praised. . . .

"Food is gold, when bought out of a wretched Arab bazaar, into which five thousand troops and their followers press to satisfy hunger. We paid eighteenpence this morning for as much milk as sufficed for three cups of tea. We had not enjoyed such a luxury for many days. . . .

"Sir James Outram commands in chief both naval and military forces, the troops being all under my immediate orders. He and I are the best friends.

"H. has supplied me with writing materials out of his sabre tache, and I scribble on the back of a small looking-glass. H. H."

Little need was there for the statement in his next communication, that his soul and mind were young and fresh. The fact is obvious at a glance. Memory was in full activity; humour interspersed pleasant illustrations, and faith was as cheerful as the lark. Of the light that was sown for the righteous he was in full participation.

"CAMP, MOHAMMERAH, *Sunday, April* 5, 1857.

"I woke this morning, and found myself sixty-two years of age, feeling, by the blessing of God, as strong or stronger than at fifty-two.

"I had organised my troops for church parade, when Sir James Outram rode down to inform me that our occupation was gone, peace having been signed with Persia on the 4th of March at Paris.

"The intelligence, which elevates some and depresses others, finds me calm in my reliance on that dear Redeemer who has watched over and cared for me, even when I knew Him not, these threescore and two years. We all wear beards here, and nearly every hair on my head and face is as gray as my first charger; but my soul and mind are young and fresh. . . .

"Love to the children."

The power of association was a great characteristic of Havelock's mind. Incidents occurring at Mohammerah reminded him of what had happened years before at Cabool, and the recollection led him to renew the expression of his gratitude to God.

The mention of his eldest son with such grateful satisfaction, will remind the reader of a similar mention of his second son in a letter which will be found in Chapter VII.

"MOHAMMERAH, *May* 1, 1857.

"In this encampment your letter of the 10th of March reached me, with one for H. He has now gone out to survey in an island called Abadan, and his work will occupy him ten days at least, which I reckon a gloomy period, his presence being the earthly accident of my existence most cheering to me. From all the rest of you I am separated by considerations of stern duty. I am most thankful when at intervals his employments enable me to see *him* twice a day.

"Our campaign has been abruptly terminated by the treaty signed on the 4th of March at Paris. Until it is ratified by the King of Persia, we are instructed to remain here. Meanwhile the weather has waxed warm, and I am reminded of my tent in the mulberry grove at Cabool in August and September 1841. Can I forget the mercy that has shielded and guided me since that time?"

On the conclusion of this brief campaign, in "a field force Order," dated "Camp, Mohammerah, May 9, 1857," the Lieutanant-General speaks with warm approval of "the entire absence of crime amongst so large a body of troops, scarcely one instance of misconduct on the part of any individual having been brought to his notice."

General Outram offered his sincere thanks also "to all now about to return to India, especially to Brigadier-General Havelock, C.B., for the zealous and valuable assistance he has afforded him at all times in command of the Second Division."

Not only of his immediate relatives was the Brigadier-General mindful, amidst his onerous military occupations. To hear from an old friend, whatever his condition in life, was a pleasure to him.

Always ready was he to send kindly and suitable replies. An instance of this kind may be mentioned:—

On his way up the Euphrates, Havelock received a letter from his old acquaintance, Sergeant Godfrey, now a yeoman warder in the Tower of London.

It had occurred to Godfrey to write to his former commander exactly at the termination of the old year 1856 and the beginning of 1857. The communication reached Havelock in due time, and received the following reply:—

"Camp, Mohammerah, Persia,
May 4, 1857.

"My good Friend Godfrey,—Your letter of the 31st of December 1856 and 1st January 1857 must no longer remain unanswered.

"You probably expected that it would find me at Calcutta or Simla, in my post as Adjutant-General of Her Majesty's Forces; but God had willed it otherwise.

"When it was put into my hand I was near the mouth of the mighty Euphrates, on board of the steamer *Berenice*, which was crowded with troops destined for the attack on this place.

"The fact is, that, about the end of last year, I received a most unexpected summons from the Bombay Government, offering me the command, with the rank of Brigadier-General, of a division of their troops, which was about to proceed to the Gulf of Persia to co-operate with the force already landed at Bushire.

"I made a hasty, or rather harassing journey, from Agra to my former location at Bombay, and my troops were in course of time despatched to seize this position, situate at the junction of the Karoon river with the Euphrates, where the Persians had thrown up rather formidable works.

"Our attack took place on the 26th of March, but the gentlemen in blue—the sailors—had all the fight to themselves.

"Their 64-pounders in about four hours so fearfully hammered and pounded the entrenchments, that a Persian Prince of the blood, who had come down with a considerable force of troops and cannon, would not look at my soldiers, but, as soon as they landed in the date groves, put himself in full retreat. Having about five miles the start of us, he was soon out of reach, taking with him, however, only five out of thirty pieces of cannon.

"My eldest son, Harry, was with me, employed in the Quartermaster-General's department, and was, as a young soldier, of course much disappointed at not seeing a fight on shore as well as a sharp naval cannonade.

"Peace with Persia has since been concluded; but here I am, occupying the ground thus won, in certainly rather hot weather, until the treaty is ratified.

"Now, I must tell you how much pleasure it has

given me to hear that your wife and you are well, and that your dear parents are still spared to you. What mercies have followed us for such a series of years!

"My family are still on the Rhine, in Germany. My eldest son is here. Joshua is in very good civil employ at Ranul Pindee, in the Punjaub.

"I had the pleasure of attending on Mr Leslie's ministry at Calcutta from February to September 1856.

"I have been kept in very fair health, in sometimes rather rough work in this country, though I am now sixty-two.—With kind regards to your wife, believe me, your sincere friend,

"H. Havelock."

"God had willed it otherwise!" The acknowledgment of God in all his ways comes out again. Why should he complain? By this time, had nothing disturbed his arrangements, he would have had a cheerful domestic home, with the ten thousand coveted enjoyments which nothing but that could bring. It seemed good to his heavenly Father to deprive him of what he looked for, and he had learned therewith to be content.

"Mercies have followed us," said he to his faithful comrade at Jellalabad. "What mercies!"

Ministry at Calcutta, too, must needs be mentioned—the ministry of Mr Leslie; ministry in which he had had pleasure.

Then Godfrey's wife, whom he had met in their worship in India, must be remembered, and the old folks, "your dear parents," must come in for a word. He was not absolutely robust just then; but the health, considering the rough work, was "very fair." An old friend's letter "must no longer remain unanswered," though one of them was Brigadier-General at Mohammerah, and the other a warder in the Tower of London.

An instance of the personal bravery, for which Havelock was famous, occurred during this Persian expedition. As the steamer was moving upwards, he saw that they must be exposed to a heavy cannonade from a fort within reach that was bristling with cannon. He ordered his men to lie down flat on the deck, and then took his own station on the paddle-box, that he might act as the emergency required. The danger to himself was imminent, for there came all around him a perfect shower of balls; but he escaped unhurt. He was not touched.

Fearlessness of this kind had become habitual to him. In part, probably, it was the result of constitutional temperament, but in a far greater measure it was the consequence of his active realisation of the power and sovereignty of God. He was no believer in casualty or chance. The well-known characteristic of the Ironsides of Cromwell distinguished Havelock remarkably. Belief in Providence possessed his soul. Confidence in Divine purposes had taken hold upon him. Of God's immediate and special and personal superintendence over every one who put his trust in Him, he had no kind of doubt. Of more value was he himself than many sparrows. Not one of them fell to the ground without his Father; much less should he ever fall there, except as it had been wisely and graciously ordained. Of the fanaticism which was satisfied with referring everything to fate, he would have been heartily ashamed; in the moral courage which sheltered itself beneath the shadow of the Almighty, he was always ready to rejoice.

CHAPTER IX.

HAVELOCK'S TIMELY RETURN TO INDIA.

DURING the Brigadier's absence in Persia a fearful calamity had happened to our Indian empire. A mutiny, which has no parallel in our former oriental history, had broken out, threatening the ignominious and final expulsion of the British race from Hindoostan.

The fears formerly expressed by Lord Metcalfe and many other officials, were apparently about to be realised, that "some fine morning all Europeans in India would get up with their throats cut!" "The flash of lightning" which Sir Charles Napier had anticipated, and for which, years ago, Sir Colin Campbell had been prepared, had fallen with terrific power, and was doing its deadly work.

The Mohammedans had called upon the Hindoos to resent all attacks upon their caste, and the Hindoos had exasperated the Mohammedans to make war upon the enemies of their faith. The army was very much within their power; and were they for once to make common cause, the Christian intruders upon their country would be destroyed, or at least expelled.

Many circumstances favoured the attempt. A cartridge had been introduced which required from the Pagan and the Mussulman personal contact with animal substances which they professed to abhor; and although only very partially introduced, it was represented as an offence against their religious prejudices that it was incumbent on them to resist.

Then, a prediction had been generally circulated that the year 1857 was the predestined year for the overthrow of the British rule. The English had been the conquerors, at the battle of Plassey, a century ago: but their doom was sealed by fate, and now there was no chance for them—they must lick the dust!

That they had taken violent possession of the country originally, was not the especial ground of complaint; nor that they had often perpetrated oppressions of which a civilised government should have been ashamed. The charge was avowedly this—that they were desiring and plotting the overthrow of the Hindoo and the Mohammedan faith. To no purpose were the protestations of the Government through their different channels of communication, and in vain was all appeal to palpable facts, such as the notorious indifference of the rulers of India to the propagation of the Christian religion, and wholly unavailing were the assurances of the missionaries that the gospel disowned all manner of compulsion;

that there was no possibility of making men the disciples of Jesus, but by their being fully persuaded in their own minds. The disaffected were sure that there was a conspiracy to substitute, by force, the stranger's faith for their own, and they would fight for it. They looked upon it as a crisis. The era had dawned for trampling the Feringhees under foot. The curse was upon them. The hour had arrived to strike the blow.

Effectively was the blow struck. Serious from the first, every day the catastrophe became more alarming. Regiment after regiment of the native troops abandoned its allegiance to the British Crown, and in some cases, amidst dreadful atrocities, put all Europeans to the sword. At Meerut, Delhi, Ferozepore, Allyghur, Lucknow, Nurseerabad, Bareilly, Shahjehanpore, and many other places, the rebels were, more or less, triumphant, and it seemed as if no alternative remained now but for the English ignobly to retire. The infection was spreading on all sides, and treasure and ammunition daily fell into the hands of the mutineers, while the stronghold at Delhi had, for the time being, become their own.

The panic at Calcutta was immense. Not only were communications constantly arriving of disaster upon disaster up the country, but discovery was made of a conspiracy to murder every European in the city. It is said that a company of sailors, having summarily ejected some natives from a carriage in which they were riding, found at the bottom of the carriage a paper which led to the revelation of the plot, and to the detection of the traitors. At all events, the ex-King of Oude, who was residing there, was suspected of being an intriguer against the Government, and he was put forthwith under arrest. Regiments in the neighbourhood were disarmed, lest, with arms and ammunition at their command, they might attempt to accomplish the designs which had, somewhat accidentally, rather, most providentially, been brought to light.

"Whilst the work of disarming," says the *Friend of India*, "was going on at Barrackpore, precisely the same process was being carried through at Calcutta, where it was rumoured that murder and mutiny were triumphant at the former place, and that a strong force of rebels was marching down upon the city from Delhi. The infection of terror raged through all classes. Chowringhee and Garden Reach were abandoned for the fort and the vessels in the river. The shipping was crowded with fugitives, and in houses which were selected as being least likely to be attacked hundreds of people gladly huddled together, to share the peculiar comfort which the presence of crowds imparts on such occasions. The hotels were fortified; bands of sailors marched through the thoroughfares, happy in the expectation of possible fighting, and the certainty of grog. Every group of natives was scanned with suspicion. The churches and the course were abandoned for the evening. A rising of either Hindoos or Mussulmans, or perhaps of both, was looked upon as certain to happen in the course of the night. From Chandernagore, the whole body of European and East-Indian inhabitants emigrated to Calcutta. The *personnel* of Government, the staff of the army, all, in short, who had anything to lose, preferred to come away and run the risk of losing it, rather than encounter the unknown danger. Many years must elapse before the night of the 14th June 1857 will be forgotten in Calcutta. There is reason to believe that the natives were equally afraid of being slaughtered by the Europeans, and as much rejoiced at finding their necks sound on the following morning."

Day after day brought fresh occasion for the belief that the whole Bengal army would be presently in revolt. Not at all improbable was it felt to be that the native independent princes would confederate with the mutineers. The refuse of the gaols, and the masses always ready for rapine and violence, were in league with them already. Though there was hope that ultimately they would be repulsed, and order be restored, yet for the time, men's hearts failed them for fear. Perhaps, in retribution for our violations of the true and the equitable and the religious, God was about severely to punish us. We had often boasted of our prowess and our power; it was not impossible that He would make us know that all such boasting is vain. Imminent, beyond any former precedent, was our jeopardy in the East. A little more, and our adversaries would be triumphant. The crisis was rapidly culminating. Peradventure for a time we must endure defeat.

At this juncture, Havelock providentially reached Bombay, on his way back from Persia. There he heard of the revolt by which India was convulsed, and determined at once that he would proceed across the country by land to head-quarters, losing no time in taking his post as Adjutant-General of the Queen's troops, which he still retained.

The following letter to Mrs Havelock informs us of his first acquaintance with what had happened:—

"MALABAR POINT, BOMBAY, *May* 31, 1857.

"I arrived here from the Persian Gulf the day before yesterday, in time to receive the astounding intelligence that the native regiments had mutinied at Meerut, and that the fortress of Delhi was in the hands of the mutineers, whilst disaffection seemed everywhere spreading in the upper provinces. My first impulse was to rejoin General Anson with all possible despatch; but after a full consultation with Lord Elphinstone and Colonel Melvill, I came to the conclusion that the route by India was in no sense safe; that I could not get through without an escort, and that none could be spared me. So H. and I embark to-morrow in the *Erin* for Pointe-de Galle. The 78th Highlanders, and 64th Queen's, which but yesterday formed part of my division at

Mohammerah, were sent round to Calcutta without landing, and a regiment summoned from Ceylon. This is the most tremendous convulsion I have ever witnessed, though I was in the thick of Cabool affairs. But the same kind Providence will watch over me now. Calcutta is in alarm, and we are here almost denuded of British troops, so I know not what to expect to hear if I get round to Calcutta. General Anson is marching on Delhi, but waits for a battering train from Philour. This morning they telegraph us from Agra that they have been compelled to disarm the native regiments. The crísis is eventful; for General Anson cannot be before Delhi until the 9th proximo, and meanwhile, the military insurrection, for such it is, gains strength."

In concurrence with Lord Elphinstone's decision, he embarked on the 1st of June, on board the *Erin*, for Galle, intending to take the next steamer thence to Calcutta. The voyage to Ceylon promised fairly at first, but during the evening of the fourth day it became stormy, and the vessel in the course of the ensuing night got aground, and struck so heavily that all hope that she would be saved was taken away.

"After the first shock," says Captain Hunt, "the ship had glided into deep water again, and all were expecting her to go down by the head, as the fore part of the vessel had at once filled, when she struck again and again, and finally gave one long surge, which fixed two-thirds of her length firmly upon the reef.

"This brought her up with a shock which made the whole frame shiver, and nearly jerked the masts out. The force of this may be imagined, as the speed at the time of its occurring was more than eleven knots the hour. . . . . To move about the decks became almost impossible, as every surge rolling in lifted the ship bodily, and, receding, dashed her with violence against the bottom. It therefore became necessary to hang on to the sides or rigging for life; and heavy rain commencing again to fall made the long hours until daylight wearisome and trying in the extreme.

"No persuasions could induce the Lascar crew to go aloft to remove the heavier sails or send the upper masts and yards down, and, by lightening the top weight, lessen the severity of the constant shocks. Huddled in groups wherever they could find shelter, they were almost useless throughout the night. Guns were fired and blue lights burned immediately it was ascertained that the accident was without remedy. These soon gave the alarm, and brought the district judge and a crowd of fishermen and others to the beach to assist. One bold fellow swam off, though nearly drowned in the breakers alongside the ship, and returning, when sufficiently recovered, with a line, a hawser was got on shore, by which a communication was established. So soon as it was sufficiently light, canoes came off, hauled along the hawser through the surf, and the passengers were all landed in two or three trips without accident."

In the correspondence with home we have Havelock's own account of this disaster:—

"QUEEN'S HOUSE, POINTE-DE-GALLE,
June 8, 1857.

"I wrote you a long letter from on board the *Erin,* little thinking what was to be her fate. On the night of the 5th, (George's tenth birthday,) we all went to rest—turned in, in sailors' phrase—the vessel going eleven knots, moonlight bright, and the weather fine. I was awoken a little before one in the morning by rain coming in at the port. I rose and shut it. In a few minutes I felt a shock, which induced me to think the vessel on shore. Another followed, which convinced me it was even so; but my mind rejected the idea, as I confided in the good look-out kept by the officers of the great Peninsular and Oriental Company. The next moment H., who had been sleeping on deck, came very calmly into my cabin, and said, 'Sir, get up, the ship has struck!' Then ensued an awful scene. The captain sprung from his bed quite overcome by the misfortune; the crew had lost their wits, and obeyed no orders. Indeed, few were given. Heavy bets had been made in the morning on the hour of our arrival, which much shocked me. The passengers were generally calm. We had to wait four hours for daylight, the ship perpetually experiencing heavy shocks. The madness of man threw us on shore, the mercy of God found us a soft place near *Caltura*. Passengers, and crew, and specie, all saved. Ship gone to pieces. Here we have arrived, all well, after some adventures, and go on as soon as our baggage arrives, in the *Fire Queen*, to Calcutta."

There was one "adventure," of which his modesty prevented him from making any mention, but which beautifully shewed that in all his ways he acknowledged God. It had devolved upon him in the emergency to assume some authority, and to address instructions to the affrighted crew. "Now, my men, if you will but obey orders, and keep from the spirit-cask, we shall all be saved." As we have been reading, they were all saved.

On the arrival of the last of the party, when he perceived that none of them had been drowned, Havelock called on them to acknowledge the goodness of the Lord in their escape. There was respectful attention, and he himself poured out the common thanksgiving for their deliverance from a watery grave.

It was "the mercy of God that had found for them a soft place," instead of rocks, where, by the earlier breaking up of the ship, they must have lost their lives. That mercy ought gratefully to be acknowledged. He would, as he did, give audible expression to their united praise.

Another instance this of his habitual recognition of the Divine Providence. Another instance also of his readiness to confess Christ before men. Not enough was it that he perceived, and that he acknowledged the interposition of Almighty Power for their rescue, he felt bound to say that he perceived and acknowledged it. If there were other godly ones among the group, they would gladly have fellowship with him in the exercise of praise. If there were undecided and wavering ones there, they would be reproved and encouraged by his avowal of Christian principle. If there were irreligious ones there, they would be admonished as to their own duty, and would be constrained to hold in honour the men who were thus steadfastly and spontaneously faithful to their religious vows.

So full was the father of homely attachments and sympathies, that in perils by the sea, and with wars and rumours of wars impending, they could not be repressed. He remembered "it was George's tenth birthday." God bless the boy!

On the 7th of June he embarked on board the *Fire Queen* for Calcutta. At Madras they took on board Lieutenant-General Sir Patrick Grant, who had been appointed to the provisional command of the army in Bengal. On the passage he accounted to Mrs Havelock for his having missed one mail.

"STEAMER 'FIRE QUEEN,' *June* 15, 1857.

"I had not a moment's time to write from Madras, but shall be able to despatch this by the steamer of the 20th, from Calcutta. At Madras we got the melancholy intelligence of the death, after a short illness, at Umballa, on the 26th May, of General

Anson. Thus my friends are snatched from me! for I think he was as kindly disposed towards me as poor Lord Frederick Fitzclarence. . . . . I keep hoping, though of course a loser by the smash of our baggage on the Ceylon coast. We should be thankful for our lives, so mercifully spared. The vessel lasted until four P.M. If she had broken up before daylight, probably few of us would have reached the shore.

"Our troops have gained advantages over the mutineers at Delhi; but the city was still in their hands, by the last accounts, and much remained to be done. Sir Henry Barnard was commanding."

On the 17th of June the two Generals arrived in Calcutta, and Havelock without any delay placed himself at the disposal of the Commander-in-Chief. Invaluable were the services of such a man. His arrival just then was auspicious in the extreme. His knowledge of the country; his acquaintance with the habits and customs of the people; his military genius and experience, especially his most trustworthy character and high standing with the soldiery, rendered him of highest worth for the emergency.

Not an hour was lost, as his last letter despatched from Calcutta to Bonn testifies:—

"United Service Club, Calcutta,
Sunday, *June* 21, 1857.

"I have barely time to tell you, by the after packet which leaves to-day, that I was yesterday re-appointed Brigadier-General, and leave by dawk as soon as possible, for Allahabad. Sir Patrick Grant lost no time in recommending me for this important command, the object of which is to relieve Cawnpore, where Sir Hugh Wheeler is threatened, and support Lucknow, where Sir Henry Lawrence is somewhat pressed. May God give me wisdom and strength to fulfil the expectations of Government, and restore tranquillity in the disturbed provinces!"

In this spirit of religiousness did he set out on his last eventful campaign. He knew what confidence was placed in him. He was aware of his competency for the undertaking. He held gratefully in mind the courage and sagacity of many of his older comrades. Various considerations cheered him, though the enterprise was hazardous; but "tranquillity in the disturbed provinces would be secured only through Divine interposition." "Wisdom and strength" adequate to the extremity could be obtained from God alone. Hence he prepared to leave for Allahabad, as seeing Him who is invisible. He would go in the strength of the Lord. The Divine sovereignty had ordered his return when his services were urgently required. In the Divine faithfulness and power he would implicitly put his trust. The work had been given him to do. The Lord graciously helping him, it should be done.

CHAPTER X.

CAWNPORE AND LUCKNOW.

In discharging the task we have prescribed for ourselves, we have hitherto confined our narrative to the barest indications of the movements in Havelock's eventful life wherever duty called him. Chiefly under his own guidance we have followed him, finding him always the same Christian soldier "without fear and without reproach," the same affectionate husband and father, and the same faithful friend. If any characteristic has been prominently outstanding, without doubt it has been his uniform submission to Duty. From the hour when he first recognised the command of God to believe in the Lord Jesus Christ, he had, without grudging, so habitually surrendered himself to all the obligations which the submission involved, that at length obedience became habitual. The effect of this discipline upon his worldly profession—upon the calling wherein he had been called—was manifest. He did not wait until the path of duty presented itself broadly before him; he was ever on the outlook for its earliest intimation. Let him but be convinced that his feet were treading there, and no consideration whatever would induce him either to leave it himself or to suffer those under his command to do so.

At no period of his history was this prominent attribute of his character, combined with his unwearied and resolute perseverance, more clearly seen than in his last campaign. And now that the shadows are gathering in the horizon, and a few short months will see this man of God lay himself down to die, we feel that we can scarcely do justice even to this brief biographical sketch if we do not shortly recapitulate the chief incidents in his last campaign.

The Kingdom of Oude had long given successive Governors-General cause for much anxiety and apprehension. Situated in the very heart of our possessions, peopled by three millions of the most military race in India, and governed by Princes whose ferocious licentiousness made the Court of Lucknow a byword and a shame, its annexation had for some time been considered by those who had watched the progress of our rule in India only a question of time. That time arrived at last, and early in 1856 Oude became a part of British India.

The appointment of Chief Commissioner was necessarily a subject of much solicitude. The righteousness and the policy of the annexation had been called in question somewhat severely, and though deemed capable of effective vindication, there was no doubt that it would involve most serious consequences, and require from the representative of British authority qualities of the highest order. Sir Henry Lawrence was a man whose judgment, cool determination, and thorough knowledge of the Asiatic character, rendered his appointment to the chief commissionership desirable, if not, indeed, imperative. In the spring of 1857 the offer of the post was made to him. With Lawrence, as with Havelock, to recognise his duty was to do it, and, though on leave of absence on account of sickness, he at once returned to Bengal, and became Chief Commissioner of Oude.

Lucknow pre-eminently needed such a man. Sagacious, wise, and determined; bold or conciliatory, as the occasion needed; his Christianity never obtruded, but never concealed; he was possessed of the qualities which rendered him peculiarly fitted to represent the Government at a court as distinguished for its adherence to all the traditions of old Mohammedanism, as for its shameless exhibition of the worst attributes of the Asiatic character.

The position next in importance to Lucknow was the military station of Cawnpore. Midway between Lucknow and Allahabad, its situation as the key of Oude, as well as other advantages, had attracted to it many merchants and traders, who, with the civil and military servants of the Company, formed a considerable European community. Here, also, a wise appointment was made. Sir Hugh Wheeler, a veteran of more than fifty years' experience, a brave old soldier, and as good as he was brave, who had won laurels in many a hard-fought field under Lord Lake, was appointed to the military command. In Lucknow and in Cawnpore the Government had put the right men in the right place.

Lucknow, the capital of Oude, is one of the largest cities in India. Extending for more than four miles on the right bank of the river Goomtee, it comprehends within its vast area the palace of the King, with its gardens, and many minor palaces, the dwellings of the princes and nobles. The Residency, now so famous, lies, like the palace of the King, between the city and the banks of the Goomtee. It is very extensive, and, with the outhouses and other buildings, covers a considerable space, in some places overlooking the city. Near it is the Muchhee Bhowun, a strong castle-like building, and on the opposite bank of the river are the cantonments. The streets are narrow and tortuous; so narrow, indeed, that the elephants, which were kept in large numbers by the Court, found some difficulty in passing. The population, said to be about three hundred thousand, was wild and lawless in the last degree,—every man armed in some way or other, and most of them ready for mischief of any kind or to any extent.

Sir Henry Lawrence, early in May, became aware

of the mutinous intentions of the native troops at Lucknow. With that foresight and sagacity for which he was so distinguished, he began immediate preparations. He requested to be invested with the chief military as well as the chief civil command. This was immediately granted, and without delay his authority was turned to good account. He found under his command little more than 500 European troops, while the native regiments numbered nearly ten times as many. Not a day was lost. He put the Residency into a state of defence, stored it with provisions, and fortified the Muchhee Bhowun. He then awaited the storm, whose omens had been darkening at every step. He had not long to wait. About the 24th the first indications were heard, and he immediately removed the sick, with the women and children, into the *enciente* of the Residency. On the 30th, Sir Henry witnessed the fierce precursors of massacre and bloodshed, and before the end of June, not only the capital, but the province, from one end to the other, was up in fierce rebellion. It may justly be a question whether in other provinces the disaffection had not been confined to the army, but unhappily in Oude it admits of no discussion. Here, under the leadership of every petty prince or landowner, bands of ruthless brigands were led on to every conceivable excess, scouring the land in search of Europeans, and butchering them with horrid cruelty.

In the hope of intercepting a large body of mutineers from Fyzabad, on the 29th of June Sir Henry issued from the Residency towards Chinnahut with such forces as he could command. Induced, most unhappily, to proceed further than he intended, he discovered, when too late, that the strength of the enemy was five times as large as he had been informed. The odds were immense, and, to add to his anxiety, his native artillery proved traitors. They cut the traces of the guns, overturned them into ditches or rendered them otherwise unserviceable, and fled to swell the ranks of the enemy. Outflanked by a powerful body of the infantry and cavalry of the mutineers, Sir Henry was compelled to retire, which, however, he could not effect without serious loss. With diminished numbers, and with an enemy increasing every day, the gallant chief felt the necessity of narrowing his line of defence. On the evening of the 1st of July orders were telegraphed to the officer in charge to fire the magazine and abandon the Muchhee Bhowun. This was accomplished without loss. The little garrison then shut themselves into the Residency, and began a defence which, for skill, endurance, and heroic bravery, is perhaps without a parallel in the annals of war.

While these events were taking place at Lucknow, the situation of Cawnpore was becoming daily a cause of equal anxiety. Accounts of the disaster at Meerut had reached Sir Hugh Wheeler about the 17th of May, and, like his chief, Sir Henry Lawrence, he began to apprehend the worst. Though brave as a lion, he was apprehensive, for he had under his charge not only the European residents, but the families of Her Majesty's 32d, then at Lucknow, while to defend them against more than three thousand sepoys and the fierce rabble that filled the town, he had at first only about sixty artillerymen and the officers of the native regiments, until reinforced by eighty-four men of the 32d, sent from Lucknow, all that Lawrence could spare. What preparations time admitted of were immediately made. Under all the circumstances, the European barracks and hospital buildings seemed to be the most eligible places for shelter, and these he immediately occupied, surrounding them with such earthworks and defences as the exigencies of the moment allowed.

While this was being done, treachery was weaving its coils around the gallant old General and his helpless charge. Nana Sahib, a perfidious miscreant, who had begun his career of crime by forging the will of his late benefactor and robbing his widow of her inheritance, resided in great splendour at Bithoor, about six miles from Cawnpore. His *quasi* civilisation, and the hospitality that his ill-gotten gains enabled him to display, as well as the stake which his great wealth seemed to give him in the continuance of the British rule, had won for him the confidence of Mr Hillersdon, the Collector of Cawnpore. To him he expressed in most emphatic terms his sympathy with the Government, and his willingness to aid it to the utmost of his power. In an evil hour he was listened to. It was arranged that he should raise a force of 1500 fighting men, with which he would be ready to stamp out the first symptoms of mutiny that might appear among the garrison of Cawnpore.

On the night of the 21st, Sir Hugh Wheeler received information that danger was imminent. All the Europeans were at once gathered into the barracks. The attempt to remove the treasure to a place of safety having been opposed by the sepoys, Nana Sahib offered his services to protect it. This was acceded to, and now having no further need of concealment, he threw off the mask, and declaring himself an enemy, announced his intention to attack the barracks. Then commenced a defence distinguished as signally for its heroism and patient endurance, as for the hideous catastrophe with which it closed.

The attack was directed in person by Nana Sahib. His force, increased hourly by the arrival of mutineers from Allahabad and other stations, and by the accession of all the brigands and armed rabble of the district, was at least ten times that of Sir Hugh Wheeler. Every building that could from any point command the barracks was crowded with sepoys, who poured a constant stream of musketry upon the devoted garrison, while the artillery hurled their deadly missiles upon the frail buildings now no longer able to shelter them. Their sufferings were fearful. The sick and wounded, men, women, and children, were crowded together into the smallest possible space; and this, under the burning heat of an Indian summer, occasioned the keenest torture. The wind came like hot air from a furnace. All necessaries were supplied in the smallest rations, and water failed them. The only well was in the entrenchments. No water could be drawn except in the evening, after the firing had ceased. That was the solitary opportunity when, in darkness and with greatest haste, they could bury their dead. It was the employment of every night, for no day passed without its deaths. All ages and all classes had one common grave—an old well out in one of the entrenchments. There the survivors placed hurriedly the body of child or wife; the rugged soldier and the lady who till near her death had never known fatigue, had one mournful burial. Few escaped from that bloody siege. But there have been preserved diaries and memoranda the most affecting that have ever been written, and letters full of comfort to those who were living in peace, from writers who were hourly drawing near to torture and to death.

Each day brought its struggle. Twice the little garrison sallied forth and spiked the guns of their opponents. Upon the 13th of June the barracks, in which all the women of the 32d Regiment and the wounded were placed, were set on fire by shells from the enemy's artillery. Four thousand sepoys came in on all sides to prevent the soldiers from saving the wounded or suppressing the flames. They were, however, driven back, but many wounded men perished. Similar assaults were continued and repulsed during the subsequent week. In one of them the besiegers lost 200 men, and although they had reduced the fire of the garrison to two guns, their losses were very great every day.

This crushing bombardment was continued until the 24th of June. The supply of water had now failed. The solitary well was dry. The only food in store was served out in half rations. The wounded died from want, and gentle spirits sank and passed away from very agony at the scene around them.

All hope of succour from without at length failed. The garrison, reduced by disease and death, and weakened by famine, could hold out no longer, and on the 24th terms of surrender were agreed to. Nana Sahib took a solemn oath upon the Gunga, and all the oaths besides which are held binding upon a Hindoo, that if the besieged would trust to him and surrender, they should be safely conveyed to the river, and sent down to Allahabad in boats.

The capitulation was effected, and Sir Hugh Wheeler, with his comrades and his charge, left their entrenchments on the morning of the 27th of June. They entered the boats, which were awaiting to carry them ostensibly to Allahabad. Two cannon, which had been masked, were immediately run out, and opened upon the boats, while the sepoys who lined the banks poured on the soldiers and their helpless wards a murderous fire. The native boatmen deserted them at once, but a few of the boats escaped to the opposite bank. They were met there by sepoys and by Oude cavalry, and all except one boat-load were seized. The men were either drowned, or shot in the river, or carried back before Nana Sahib, and massacred by these savages in his presence, while the children and women were shut up for the present in one building. The boat that escaped struck upon a sand-bank on the 28th. Sepoys who had followed its course instantly fired upon the passengers. Fourteen officers and soldiers fought them desperately, and got clear away; but they lost their road, and were obliged to take refuge in a temple. From their shelter they were inhumanly smoked out. They then again fought the sepoys, and five of them escaped to the Ganges. By hard swimming with the current, four left their pursuers behind them, and at a distance of seven miles from the spot where they had taken the water, they were rescued by the servants of a friendly Rajah, and finally saved.

A sadder story than this of Cawnpore is not told in all our history. The butchery of the men, the confinement and subsequent murder of the women and children, form a triumph of cruel perfidy. The defence of the Cawnpore entrenchments was a noble feat of heroism in a heroic time—a defence by four hundred and fifty against four thousand, and at last against ten thousand men. Deprived of water, straitened for food, weary and wounded, the soldiers would have dashed recklessly through the ranks around them, but they were restrained by pity for the number of women and children whom they defended. Betrayed in the end by treachery, which many of them had dreaded from the first, these men, in the midst of an agonising parting, sought no favour from their murderer, except, indeed, one through Mr Moncrieff, the Chaplain of Cawnpore, and that was for time to pray. They read and prayed, "shook hands all round"—the old General and his followers—and then they were massacred in cold blood.

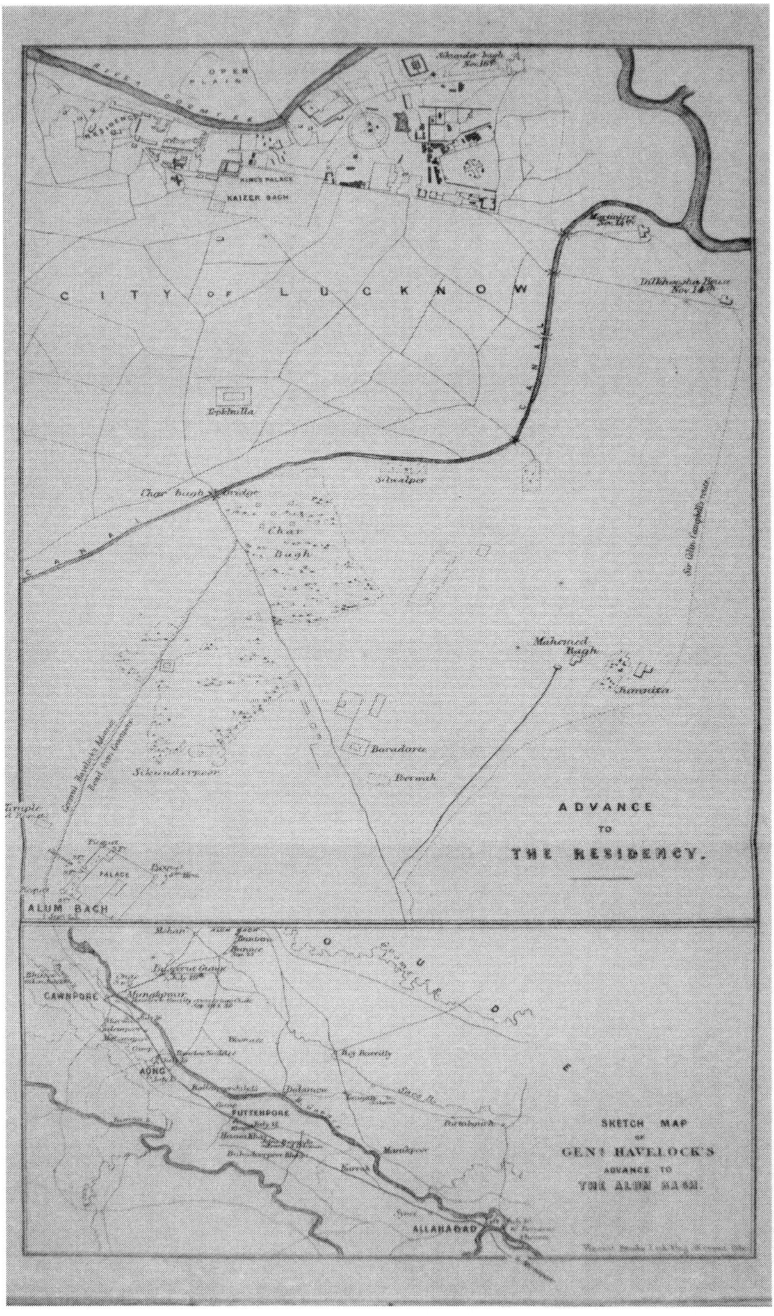
ADVANCE
TO
THE RESIDENCY.
CITY of LUCKNOW
CANAL
OPEN PLAIN
KING'S PALACE
KAIZER BAGH
Char bagh Bridge
Char Bagh
Mahomed Bagh
Baradaree
Sikunderpoor
Sir Colin Campbell's route
ALUM BAGH
PALACE
CAWNPORE
AONG
FUTTEHPORE
ALLAHABAD
OUDE
SKETCH MAP
OF
GENL HAVELOCK'S
ADVANCE TO
THE ALUM BAGH.

CHAPTER XI.

HAVELOCK'S ADVANCE TO CAWNPORE.

ON the last day of June Havelock arrived at Allahabad, to assume the command of the relieving army. Colonel Neill, a soldier as brave and fearless as he was determined, had, by the most energetic measures, succeeded in placing that important station in comparative safety; and on that day had sent a force of 820 men under Major Renaud, in advance towards Cawnpore. While vigorous preparations were being made for the despatch of the rest of the column, news of the catastrophe at Cawnpore reached Allahabad, from Sir Henry Lawrence, at Lucknow. The following letter describes Havelock's impression of the emergency :—

"ALLAHABAD, *July* 3, 1857.

"This state of perpetual hurry and locomotion, in which I have been since leaving Calcutta, prevented my writing by the mail which will leave that port to-morrow. This is the first packet that has left these shores since I returned to India which has not carried a letter to you.

"Mutiny and treachery have been gaining ground every day since I last wrote, and you must expect to hear of great calamities. Lawrence still holds Lucknow triumphantly, but has great odds against him. It is believed that the force at Cawnpore has been entirely destroyed by treachery; having unfortunately been seduced into a treaty with its foes.

"I march to-morrow to endeavour to retake Cawnpore and rescue Lucknow."

It had been Havelock's intention to leave Allahabad on the morning of the 4th, but it was not till early on the morning of the 7th July that he began his march. His force, including Renaud's column in advance, numbered not more than a thousand Europeans, and he had only 150 Sikhs and 30 Irregular Cavalry; in all, less than 1200 men. With this column he determined to advance to the relief of the beleaguered garrisons, cutting his way through a country swarming with rebel troops, who had been well armed and disciplined by ourselves. The odds were greatly against him. But Havelock was equal to the emergency. In his Staff, Captain Beatson filled the office of Assistant-Adjutant-General, Colonel Tytler acted as Quartermaster-General, while the General's son had been taken from the adjutancy of the 10th Foot to be aide-de-camp to his father in this his first campaign.

As they passed through the streets, the Hindoos evidently regarded them with dread, while the scowl of hatred sat darkly on the averted faces of the Mohammedans, whose disloyalty was becoming every day yet better known. No time was left for minute examination of their misdeeds then, and Havelock hurried on to join the detachment under Major Renaud.

The rain fell fast and heavy; the fields on each side of the Grand Trunk Road were turned into morasses. Here and there the blackened ruins of destroyed bungalows told how rebellion had done its work, while the bodies of rebels hanging from the trees by the roadside marked Renaud's path of retribution. For three days our men marched only the customary distance, for the heat was oppressive, and the General determined to husband the strength of his troops for the arduous struggle on which he knew they were about to enter.

On the 10th Havelock saw that the position of Renaud's column, then in advance, was becoming critical. The fall of Cawnpore had freed the mutineers from occupation, and they had rapidly pushed down a force to the vicinity of Futtehpore, within five miles of which the Major would arrive on the morning of the 12th. He would thus be exposed to the attack of 3500 rebels with twelve guns.

No time was to be lost. Accordingly, on the 10th, Havelock marched, under a broiling sun, fifteen miles to Synee; and, resuming his course at eleven o'clock at night, joined Major Renaud on the road by moonlight, and with him marched to Khaga, five miles from Futtehpore, where, soon after dawn, he took up a position. There were now 1400 British bayonets and eight guns, assisted by a small native force. The General's information had been better than that of the enemy, for when Lieutenant-Colonel Tytler pushed a reconnaissance up to the town they evidently supposed that they had only Major Renaud's little but gallant force in their front. After firing on the Colonel and his escort, they pushed forward two guns and a force of infantry and cavalry, cannonading his front, and threatening his flanks.

Havelock, wishing earnestly to give his harassed soldiers rest, waited until this ebullition should expend itself, making no counter-disposition beyond posting 100 Enfield Riflemen of the 64th in an advanced copse. But the enemy maintained his attack with the audacity which his first supposition had inspired, and which the General's apparent inertness fostered. He saw that it would injure the *morale* of his troops to permit them thus to be bearded, and he determined at once to bring on an action.

Futtehpore constituted a position of no small strength. The hard, dry Grand Trunk Road subdivides it, and it was the only means of convenient travel, for the plains on both sides are covered at this season by accumulations of water to the depth of two, three, and four feet. It is surrounded by garden enclosures of great strength, with high walls, and has within it many houses of good masonry.

In front of the swamps were hillocks, villages, and mango groves, which the enemy had already occupied in force.

The General's disposition was immediately made. The guns, now eight in number, were formed on and close to the road, in the centre, under Capt. Maude, of the Royal Artillery, protected and aided by 100 Enfield Riflemen of the 64th. The detachments of infantry were, at the same moment, thrown into line of quarter-distance column, at deploying distance, and thus advanced in support, covered by Enfield skirmishers. The small force of Volunteers and Irregular Cavalry moved forward on the flanks, on harder ground.

The action was soon decided. In a short time the spirit of the enemy seemed utterly subdued; the rifle fire, reaching them at an unexpected distance, filled them with dismay; and when Captain Maude was enabled to push his guns through flanking swamps to point-blank range, his surprisingly accurate fire demolished their little remaining confidence. In a moment three guns were abandoned on the roadway, and the force advancing steadily, drove the enemy before it at every point.

Major Renaud won a hillock on the right in good style, and struggled on through the inundation. The 78th, in extension, kept up his communication with the centre; the 64th gave strength to the centre and left; while, on the left, the 84th and the Sikh Regiment of Ferozepore pressed back the enemy's right.

As Havelock moved forward, the enemy's guns continued to fall into his hands, and then in succession the sepoys were driven by skirmishers and columns from the garden enclosures, from a strong barricade on the road, and from the town-wall, into, through, and beyond the town. They endeavoured to make a stand a mile on the other side of it, while our troops were in such a state of exhaustion that the General almost despaired of driving the enemy further. At the same time, the mutineers of the 2d Light Cavalry made an effort to renew the combat by charging, with some success, our Irregular Horse, whose intentions throughout the fight had been worse than doubtful. But, to prevent mischief, the guns and riflemen were, with great labour, pushed again to the front. Their fire soon put the enemy to final and irretrievable flight, and Havelock, taking up his position in triumph, halted his weary men to breakfast; having marched altogether twenty-four miles, and beaten the enemy so completely, that all their ammunition, baggage, and guns were in his hands.

"I have to acquaint your Lordship," he wrote to the Governor-General, "that I have this morning attacked and totally defeated the insurgents, capturing eleven guns, and scattering their forces in utter confusion in the direction of Cawnpore. By two harassing marches I joined Major Renaud's advanced column three hours before daylight, encamped about eight o'clock four miles from Futtehpore, where, pitching our tents, the enemy advanced out of Futtehpore, and opened fire upon a reconnaissance under Colonel Tytler. I had a wish to defer the fight until to-morrow, but, thus assailed, was compelled to accept the challenge. I marched with eight guns in the centre under Captain Maude, R.A., forming the whole of the infantry in quarter-distance column in support. Captain Maude's fire electrified the enemy, who abandoned gun after gun, and were then driven by our skirmishers and column through garden enclosures and the streets of Futtehpore in complete confusion. My loss is merely nominal; not a single European touched. My column had marched twenty-four miles up to the ground I write from; Major Renaud's, nineteen miles. The conduct of the troops in sustaining the fatigue of so long a march, and enduring the heat of a frightful sun, is beyond praise. The enemy's strength is said to have been two regiments of cavalry and three of infantry, and eleven guns."

The battle of Futtehpore presented few of those remarkable incidents that distinguished subsequent fields. It was a duel of artillery and musketry at the beginning, and so continued to the end. The enemy was no match for the practice of our artillery, nor the range of the Enfield; and they fell back step by step, never getting into range with their own guns or small arms. Their cavalry at one period outflanked our army, and charged boldly through fields two feet deep with water, into the baggage on the rear. The small body of Irregular Cavalry—which must not be confounded with Havelock's brave Volunteer Cavalry—behaved badly; but the detachments of infantry received the rebel horse without forming square; and the latter, suffering from the Enfields, turned their bridles, and galloped away.

In thanking his soldiers for their arduous exertions, which produced, in four hours, the strange result of a whole army driven from a strong position, eleven guns captured, and their whole force scattered to the winds, without the loss of a single British soldier, Havelock added,—

"To what is this astonishing effect to be attributed? To the fire of the British artillery, exceeding in rapidity and precision all that the Brigadier-General has ever witnessed in his not short career; to the power of the Enfield rifle in British hands; to British pluck, that good quality that has survived the revolution of the hour; *and to the blessing of Almighty God* on a most righteous cause,—the cause of justice, humanity, truth, and good government in India."

The smoke of battle had scarcely cleared away when his thoughts reverted to his home on the Rhine. He wrote his wife:—

"FUTTEHPORE, *July* 13, 1857.

"One of the prayers oft repeated throughout my

life since my school days, has been answered, and I have lived to command in a successful action. I must refer you for the particulars to my despatch. I will here only say that I marched down upon this place yesterday morning, Sunday the 12th (battle of the Boyne) with harassed troops, intending to attack the insurgents next day, but their fate led them on. Out they sallied and insulted my camp, whereupon I determined to try an immediate action. We fought, and I may say that in ten minutes the affair was decided, for in that short time our Enfield rifles and cannon had taken all conceit of fight out of the mutineers. Amongst them was the 56th, the very regiment which I led on at Maharajpore.

"I challenged them,—'There's some of you that have beheld me fighting; now try upon yourselves what you have seen in me.'

"But away with vain glory! Thanks to Almighty God, who gave me the victory! I captured in four hours eleven guns, and scattered the enemy's whole force to the winds. I now march to retake Cawnpore, where, alas! our troops have been treacherously destroyed, and to succour Lawrence at Lucknow. . . . Norris would have rejoiced, and so would dear old Julius Hare, if he had survived to see the day. H. was in the thickest of the fight, but, God be praised, escaped unhurt. "H. H."

The heat was excessive. Twelve men had died from exposure to the scorching sun, and from sheer fatigue. Anxious as the General was to reach Cawnpore, he gladly welcomed the grateful shade of a grove of mango trees, where he rested his exhausted troops.

Justice was now done to Hikrimtoolah Khan, an old Deputy-Collector at Futtehpore. Early in the revolt all the Europeans escaped from Futtehpore, except Mr Robert Tucker, the Judge of the District. He also might have got away, but he refused to desert his house and his post. The mob surrounded him, and Hikrimtoolah Khan proposed to try him. The scheme was unsuccessful, because the stern judge would not surrender. Sixteen of his assailants fell by the hand of this brave man ere he was killed. At last the Deputy-Collector was able to shew the feet, the hands, and head of the judge to the mob as those of a traitor. Yet this ruffian came to congratulate General Havelock. He did not dream that the evidence of native Christians had been taken on his guilt. He was arrested. The time of tedious appeals to superior authorities which he remembered was past. The evidence of his guilt was conclusive, and he was executed on the spot.

On the 14th the army recommenced their onward march. That evening the General learned that the enemy were entrenched across the road at Aong, a village upon the road a few miles in advance of his position. The men bivouacked for the night; and early on the 15th, they marched upon Aong. Lieut.-Colonel Tytler, with his small body of mounted volunteers, led the way. The artillery, supported by the Madras Fusiliers, armed with the Enfield rifles, followed.

The enemy's entrenchments were not formidable, but, the country being thickly wooded, he was enabled to maintain himself for some time against Havelock's fire, during which interval large bodies of cavalry advanced on both flanks with the intention of capturing the baggage. These attacks were becoming troublesome, and to defeat them, *as he had only twenty horse,* the General was compelled to protect the flanks with the infantry in second line, and by artillery fire. "It is gratifying," he wrote, "that the enemy was unable to capture a single animal or follower. The last attempt was defeated by the baggage guards, invalids under the command of a sergeant of the 78th, whose fire was very effective. Colonel Tytler, however, at length overcame all resistance, drove the enemy before him, and captured his cannon. The road was strewed for miles with abandoned tents, ammunition, and other materials of war."

Having halted the troops for refreshment, he learned that the bridge on the Pandoo stream, which he must cross in his advance to Cawnpore, was not destroyed, but defended by guns of heavy calibre. As the passage of the river otherwise would have been difficult, to save the bridge, Havelock hastily pressed on his troops, and after a march of three miles, they reached the nullah, filling the channel with its swollen waters, like a river. The bridge was defended by artillery, and the enemy were entrenched on the opposite bank.

Measures were immediately taken to force the passage of the stream. Captain Maude having proposed to envelope it with his artillery fire, by placing three guns on the road and three on either flank, the General consented, and the whole of the Madras Fusiliers, being the most practised marksmen in the force, were then extended as Enfield riflemen. They lined the banks of the stream, and kept up a galling fire.

The enemy opened an effective cannonade upon Havelock's column as they advanced along the road. They therefore deployed, and advanced with great steadiness in parade order in support of the guns and riflemen. Captain Maude's bullets soon produced an evident effect, and then the right wing of the Fusiliers, led on by Major Renaud, gathered to the bridge, sprang over the short space between them and the foe, and followed with alacrity by the infantry in column, they captured two guns. But the mutineers did not wait for the bayonet. They fled at all points, never pausing in their race until they reached Cawnpore.

The intelligence of the defeat at the Pandoo Nuddee must have reached Nana Sahib on the night between the 15th and 16th of July, and resulted in that consummation of a series of crimes by the ruler of Bithoor which render him a disgrace to our common nature. He had before been guilty of treachery towards General Wheeler and the garrison under his command, having added the guilt of murder to the dishonour which a broken capitulation attaches to a soldier's name. On the 10th of June he ordered a lady and her three children, who came helpless fugitives to Cawnpore, to be murdered. On the 11th of June, another lady, a fugitive also, was shot, and her head sent to the Nana. On the 12th a body of fugitives from Futtyghur, numbering one hundred and thirty-six persons, chiefly females and children, were persuaded to land near Cawnpore, and having been taken to Nana Sahib, by his orders were cruelly slaughtered on the spot. But he had not yet done. The women and children of the helpless garrison, consigned to a captivity worse than death, were still in his hands. Upon these helpless prisoners he resolved to wreak his savage revenge forthwith, and ere the sun rose next morning he had perpetrated a deed of relentless cruelty to which history scarcely affords a parallel.

"He filled up the measure of his iniquities on the 15th," says Havelock, "for, on hearing that the bridge of the Pandoo Nuddee had been forced, he ordered the immediate massacre of the wives and children of our British soldiers still in his possession in this cantonment, which was carried out by his followers with every circumstance of barbarous malignity."

This horrible catastrophe will never be remembered without a shudder. Modern warfare knows nothing equal to it for deliberate barbarity. The agony of mothers and the cries of infants come back to every man who reads the cruel story; and no one can wonder that the soldiers, as they passed through Cawnpore, and saw the words written on that bloody wall by mothers in their dying anguish, should have vowed vengeance against the perpetrators of this deed of blood.

CHAPTER XII.

ENCOUNTERS WITH NANA SAHIB.

AT daybreak on the morning of the 16th, the army resumed its march. The troops were strong in hope, for a rumour had reached them on the previous night that the women and children of the murdered garrison were still alive at Cawnpore. The gallant fellows were ignorant that many of those helpless sufferers were already dead, whilst others at the time were expiring amidst the throes and throbbings of a lingering, and yet procrastinated, death!

Havelock learned that Nana Sahib had taken up a position at the village of Ahirwa, where the Grand Trunk Road unites with that which leads direct to the military cantonment of Cawnpore. It was found that his entrenchments had cut and rendered impassable both roads, and that his guns, seven in number, (two light and five siege calibre,) were disposed along his position, which consisted of a series of villages. Behind these, his infantry, consisting of mutinous troops and his own armed followers, was disposed for defence. It was evident that an attack in front would expose the British to a murderous fire from his heavy guns sheltered in his entrenchment. The General resolved, therefore, to manœuvre in order to turn the Nana's left. The camp and baggage were accordingly kept back, under proper escort, at the village of Maharajpoor, while he halted his troops there two or three hours in the mango groves to cook, and gain shelter from a burning sun.

The column then moved off, right in front. The Fusiliers led, followed by two guns; then came the Highlanders, in rear of whom was the central battery of six guns under Captain Maude. The 64th and 84th had two guns more in their rear, and the regiment of Ferozepore closed the column.

The troops, defiling at a steady pace, soon changed direction, and began to circle round the enemy's left. They were shrouded for some time by clumps of mango; but as soon as the enemy comprehended the object of their march, an evident sensation was created in his lines. He pushed forward on his left a large body of horse, and opened a fire of shot and shell from the whole of his guns. But he was evidently disconcerted by the advance on his flank, and anxious for his communication with Cawnpore. Havelock's troops continued their progress until his left was wholly opened to attack, and then forming line, advanced in direct echelon of regiments and batteries from the right. A wing of the Fusiliers again covered the advance, extended as riflemen.

"The opportunity had arrived," says Havelock, "for which I have long anxiously waited, of developing the prowess of the 78th Highlanders. Three guns of the enemy were strongly posted behind a lofty hamlet, well entrenched. I directed this regiment to advance, and never have I witnessed conduct more admirable. They were led by Colonel Hamilton, and followed him with surpassing steadiness and gallantry under a heavy fire. As they approached the village they cheered and charged with the bayonet, the pipes sounding the pibroch. Need I add that the enemy fled, the village was taken, and the guns captured."

The Highlanders had never fought in that quarter of India before, and their character was unknown to the foe. Their advance has been described by spectators as a beautiful illustration of the power of discipline.

"With sloped arms and rapid tread, through the broken and heavy lands, and through the well-directed fire of artillery and musketry, linked in their unfaltering lines, they followed their mounted leaders, the mark for many rifles. They did not pause to fire—did not even cheer; no sound from them was heard as that living wall came on and on, to conquer or to die. Now they are near the village; but their enemies occupy every house, and from every point a galling fire is poured on them from the heavy guns. The men lie down till the iron storm passes over. It was but for a moment.

The General gave the word, 'Rise up! Advance!' and wild cheers rung out from those brave lines—wilder even than their fatal fire within a hundred yards; and the pipes sounded the martial pibroch, heard so often as earth's latest music by dying men. The men sprung up the hill, covered by the smoke of their crushing volley, almost with the speed of their own bullets; over and through all obstacles, the gleaming bayonets advanced; and then followed those moments of personal struggle, not often protracted, when the Mahratta learned, too late for life, the power of the Northern arm. The position was theirs. All that stood between them and the guns fled the field or was cut down. General Havelock was with his men. 'Well done, 78th,' he exclaimed. 'You shall be my own regiment. Another charge like that will win the day.'"

"The enemy's infantry," wrote Havelock, "appeared to be everywhere in full retreat, and I had ordered the fire to cease, when a reserve 24-pounder was opened on the Cawnpore Road, which caused considerable loss to my force; and, under cover of its fire, two large bodies of cavalry at the same time riding insolently over the plain, their infantry once more rallied. The beating of their large drums, and numerous mounted officers in front, announced the definitive struggle of the Nana for his usurped dominion.

"I had previously ordered my Volunteer Cavalry to adventure a charge on a more advanced part of the enemy's horse, and I have the satisfaction to report that they conducted themselves most creditably. One of their number, Mr Carr, was killed in the charge.

"But the final crisis approached. My artillery cattle, wearied by the length of the march, could not bring up the guns to my assistance; and the 1st Madras Fusiliers, 64th, 84th, and 78th detachments, formed in line, were exposed to a heavy fire from the 24-pounder on the road. I was resolved this state of things should not last; so, calling upon my men, who were lying down in line, to leap on their feet, I directed another steady advance. It was irresistible. The enemy sent round shot into our ranks until we were within 300 yards, and then poured in grape with such precision and determination as I have seldom witnessed. But the 64th, led by Major Stirling and my aide-de-camp, who had placed himself in their front, were not to be denied. Their rear shewed the ground strewed with wounded; but on they steadily and silently came, then with a cheer charged, and captured the unwieldy trophy of their valour.

"The enemy lost all heart, and, after a hurried fire of musketry, gave way in total rout. Four of my guns came up and completed their discomfiture by a heavy cannonade; and, as it grew dark, the roofless barracks of our artillery were dimly descried in advance, and it was evident that Cawnpore was once more in our possession."

"Such," (says the author of "The Indian Mutiny,") was the battle of Cawnpore, in which 1000 British troops and 300 Sikhs, labouring under every disadvantage, a powerful sun over their heads, a merciless enemy in their front, strongly entrenched, without cavalry, and with an artillery of inferior weight, defeated 5000 native troops, armed and trained by our own officers. Perhaps in no action that ever was fought was the superior power of arrangement, moral force, personal daring, and physical strength of the European over the Asiatic more apparent. The rebels fought well; many of them did not flinch from a hand-to-hand encounter with our troops; they stood well to their guns, served them with accuracy; but yet, in spite of this, of their strong position, of their disproportionate excess in number, they were beaten."

The wounded were now gathered together and cared for. The sentries commenced their nightly watch, the over-wrought soldiers slept soundly for many hours, when a crash that shook the earth awoke them:—Nana Sahib had blown up the Cawnpore magazine, and abandoned the place!

The following General Order, issued on the morning after the battle, and one of the last General Havelock penned, must now possess a melancholy interest:—

"Cawnpore, won by Lord Lake in 1803, has been a happy and peaceful place ever since, until the wretched ambition of a man, whose uncle's life was, by a too indulgent Government, spared in 1817, filled it, in 1857, with rapine and bloodshed. When, soldiers, your valour won the bridge at the Pandoo Nuddee, you were signing the death-warrant of the helpless women and children of your comrades of the 32d. They were murdered in cold blood by the miscreant Nana Sahib, whose troops fled in dismay at the victorious shout of your line, on the evening of the memorable 16th.

"Soldiers! Your General is satisfied, and more than satisfied with you. He has never seen steadier or more elevated troops,—but your labours are only beginning. Between the 7th instant and the 16th, you have, under the Indian sun of July, marched 126 miles, and fought four actions: but your comrades at Lucknow are in peril. Agra is besieged; Delhi still the focus of mutiny and rebellion. You must make great sacrifices if you would obtain great results. Three cities have to be saved; two strong places to be disblockaded. Your General is confident that he can effect all these things, and restore this part of India to tranquillity, if you only second him with your efforts; and if your discipline is equal to your valour.

"Highlanders,—It was my earnest desire to afford you the opportunities of shewing how your predecessors conquered at Maida;—you have not degenerated. Assaye was not won by a more silent, compact, and resolute charge than was the village near Jausemow on the 16th inst.

"64th,—You have put to silence the jibes of your enemies throughout India. Your fire was reserved until you saw the colour of your enemy's mustachios,—this gave us the victory."

Havelock's account of these successive engagements, to the circle at Bonn, has a significant mention of the courage of his eldest son and a reference to his youngest brother, which will be deemed pleasant evidence of his habitual and paramount recollections of home:—

"CAWNPORE, *July* 1857.

"Last week I fought four fights. On the 12th I took Futtehpore; on the 15th I fired the village Aong and the bridge over the Pandoo Nuddee, on the 16th I recaptured this place, defeating the usurper Nana Sahib in a pitched battle, and taking all his guns. I lost a hundred men. I never saw so brave a youth as the boy H.; he placed himself opposite the muzzle of a gun that was scattering death into the ranks of the 64th Queen's, and led on the regiment, under a shower of grape, to its capture. This finished the fight. The grape was deadly, but he calm as if telling George stories about India. . . . . Lawrence had died of his wounds. . . . . Mary Thornhill," (a niece of the General's,) "is in great peril at Lucknow. I am marching to relieve it. Trust in God, and pray for us. All India is up in arms against us, and everywhere around me things are looking black. Thank God for His especial mercies to me. We are campaigning in July. "H. H."

The men of the 84th Regiment were first in Cawnpore, on the morning of. the 17th. They scoured the town for armed rebels, but none were to be found. As they prosecuted their research, however, a European rushed in among them. This was Mr Shephard, who had been sentenced some time before by Nana Sahib to work upon the roads. Afterwards he had been forgotten when others were murdered, and during the panic of the previous day he had escaped. He led the soldiers to the house of death. Rarely had men looked upon a more sickening sight. The very blood, in some places of the floor, went over the soldiers' shoes. Steeped in that they found locks of ladies' hair, leaves of religious books, the bonnets and hats of little children, and their mothers' combs, in strange confusion. Sword-cuts marked the wall low down, as if the poor victims had crouched to escape the blows; and amid them were scratched the messages of dying mothers to their countrymen. Outside the house was the well, into which the dead had been thrown for burial, and the wounded for death. Their corpses had been heaped together, and were still uncovered. The men of other regiments came up, exasperated and saddened at the mournful tidings. Rugged men, who had charged to the cannon's mouth on the previous day, wept like little children, as they turned from that spectacle of guilt and suffering. From that day each detachment and regiment as they reached Cawnpore visited the scene of murder, regarding it as Nana Sahib's challenge and defiance to a conflict of absolute extermination on one side or the other.

For General Havelock, the discovery of this well neutralised the gratification of his victory. He had pressed on to Cawnpore in the hope of opening a dungeon, and releasing helpless prisoners. He wished to restore liberty to the captive, children to their fathers, and wives to their husbands. He was a chivalrous soldier, whose sword had never been raised against the fallen. To him, therefore, these butcheries, which had given to this contest a character of blackest infamy, were cause of unspeakable grief. But he restrained himself, and, wrought upon by his influence, his army behaved well. Cawnpore was completely in their power; yet, under this terrible provocation, no hand was raised against its inhabitants, and not a single British bayonet was soiled by their blood.

When writing his despatch, with all that had just occurred pressing forcibly on his mind, Havelock thus recognises the Author and Giver of his success :—

"CAWNPORE CANTONMENT, *July* 17.

"By the blessing of God I recaptured this place yesterday, and totally defeated Nana Sahib in person, taking more than six guns, four of siege calibre. The enemy were strongly posted behind a succession of villages, and obstinately disputed for 140 minutes every inch of the ground, but I was enabled, by a flank movement to my right, to turn his left, and this gave us the victory. Nana Sahib had barbarously murdered all the captive women and children before the engagement. He has retired to Bithoor, and blew up this morning, on his retreat, the Cawnpore magazine. He is said to be strongly fortified. I have not been yet able to get in the return of killed and wounded, but estimate my loss at about seventy, chiefly from the fire of grape."

Having rested his weary troops for a single day, on the morning of the 19th General Havelock marched against Bithoor, where he had been told that Nana Sahib would defend himself desperately behind forty-five guns, with 5000 men. The threat, however, was not fulfilled. The Mahratta chief could not trust his men to defend his palace. Their courage failed them, and they fled over the Ganges, carrying off most of their guns. The General wrote:—"Nana Sahib's followers appear to be deserting him. He has fled from Bithoor, which was occupied yesterday, without resistance. Thirteen guns were found in the place. His palace is in flames. General Neill has joined me with a strong reinforcement of British soldiers. Lucknow is safe for the present."

In his short campaign from Allahabad to Bithoor, Havelock had thus taken forty-four guns, and he had gained four battles: Futtehpore, Aong, Pandoo Nuddee, and Cawnpore. But these successes are mere indications of his almost unparalleled exertions; they had been gained with a force utterly inadequate to the magnitude of the undertaking, and almost destitute of cavalry. They had been achieved, too, against fearful odds, the enemy consisting of troops disciplined and taught by ourselves to fight,—some of them Havelock's old soldiers,—well armed, strong in cavalry and artillery, and, above all, accustomed to the scorching heat of a July sun.

But these victories had cost the General men whom he could ill spare. The gallant Renaud had died of his wounds. Captain Stuart Beatson, who had been the life of his small squadron of cavalry, had succumbed to cholera. Disease and death were busy in his ranks, already decimated by the foe. Reinforcements must be obtained, or the issue might be fatal to the British arms.

On his return from Bithoor to Cawnpore, Havelock had heard with deep sorrow the tidings from Lucknow of the death of Sir Henry Lawrence. With his usual superiority to fear, Sir Henry had declined the advice of his Staff to withdraw as far as possible out of reach of the round shot and shell which were incessantly battering the Residency like a hailstorm. On the 2d July a shell, fired with too fatal precision, entered the room where he was sitting, and, bursting, wounded him so severely that he died two days afterwards. This calamity deprived the beleaguered garrison of its head, and, though bravely holding out, it was known that their danger was imminent in the extreme. This information was not needed to increase Havelock's anxiety to relieve them. He had urged Neill to join him from Allahabad with every available man —a request which that gallant soldier made every effort to fulfil. On the 20th, with 270 men, all that he could take with safety from the fort of Allahabad, he arrived ; and though these reinforcements did no more than repair the breaches made in his little army by battle and disease, Havelock determined to advance. Leaving General Neill at Cawnpore, where his presence was much needed, he began to cross the Ganges on the 21st, and on the 25th, with his gallant fifteen hundred, commenced his first march to relieve Lucknow.

CHAPTER XIII.

HAVELOCK'S FIRST ADVANCE TO LUCKNOW.

THE rainy season was at its height, and the country in a deluge. The fields on each side of the raised and straight roads were swamps, in some places deep in water. The men were not provided with an adequate supply either of tents or carriages.

On the morning of the 29th the advancing force found their foes stationed in great strength at the town of Unao. The enemy was posted in a small village between General Havelock's army and the town. The houses of the place were surrounded by walled gardens; every wall was loopholed, while a deep swamp protected the enemy's right. A narrow passage communicated between his rear and Unao, which extended for three quarters of a mile upon his left. This causeway ran through fields flooded close to the road; so that the village could only be penetrated by the road. The 78th Highlanders and the 1st Madras Fusiliers with two guns began the attack. They drove the enemy from the gardens; but when they approached the village, where every house had been extemporised into a petty garrison, a destructive fire was opened upon them. The mutineers fought with obstinate courage, but they were eventually overcome and driven back upon the town. Here they rallied, and re-formed in great strength. But Havelock was instantly upon them, and the issue was not long doubtful. Their guns were taken, their infantry and horse put to flight. During the whole of the action a large detachment of Nana Sahib's horse threatened the left flank, but without effecting any injury.

The July sun now beat fiercely on the wearied soldiers, and compelled Havelock to halt his force at Unao for three hours. Night was coming on when the enemy checked his advance by a well-directed fire from the earthworks of Busserut Gunge. This is a town walled and surrounded by deep ditches, which had been greatly strengthened by earthworks. The gate in front was defended by a round tower, mounting four heavy guns. Behind the town there runs a nullah, which being at this time full of water, could be crossed only by a narrow causeway and bridge. General Havelock ordered the 64th to turn the town on the left, and penetrate between that bridge and the enemy. The 78th and the Fusiliers rapidly carried the earthworks of the town, seized the guns, and drove out the enemy, before the 64th could take a position to intercept them.

It was now past six P.M., and the enemy could not be pursued; for even had Havelock been assisted by cavalry, they could not have operated among the swamps. That was the second time in July on which, in one day, his army had fought two battles and gained two victories. The loss of the enemy in the morning battle of Unao was estimated by the natives at 1500 men. General Havelock in his bulletin wrote—"It might in truth amount to 500 killed and wounded. It was lighter at Busserut Gunge."

That night brought many anxious considerations to Havelock's mind. These two battles had cost him 12 men killed, and 76 wounded,—a loss of 88 for the time from his limited strength. True, he had twice defeated the enemy upon their own ground, taken two of their strongholds, and nineteen of their guns; but he was far from Lucknow. One officer had been killed; two were wounded. Colonel Tytler, hardly able to keep on his horse, had set through the day an example of daring and activity; but that devotion to duty could not continue. His strength was failing fast, and he was only one of many. *Cholera, too, had begun to attack the little army.* Soldiers who had charged with irresistible power that day, at night lay down weak with disease. The army had many wounded, but they had many more sick. Their leader could not reckon on more than 1200 healthy men; and he already had nearly 300 invalids. To send the sick and wounded back to Cawnpore would require a convoy of at least 300 men. He could not spare that number from his army and still hope to reach Lucknow, which was yet thirty-six miles away. What a night of trial to Havelock's faith. Yet his despatch indicates no surrender of his confidence.

The General's resolution was taken calmly. He could not abandon the besieged in Lucknow, but neither could he leave his own sick and wounded soldiers behind. He wrote urgently for reinforcements, and then, having waited in Busserut Gunge until two in the afternoon, he fell back upon Unao, where the army passed the night. The movement at first excited some surprise among the men, who could not well understand why ground so bravely won should be at once abandoned. But they had confidence in their General, and they acquiesced without murmuring in his decision. Early next morning they marched to Mungulwar, a few miles from Unao, and there they stopped. His communication with Cawnpore, with the Ganges between, was of vital importance, and he therefore determined to hold Mungulwar. From that place he forwarded his sick and wounded back to Cawnpore.

A letter was written in the course of this depressing day, still exhibiting his unfaltering confidence in God.

"CAMP, NEAR CAWNPORE, ON THE LUCKNOW-ROAD,
July 31, 1857.

"I write to tell you that, by God's blessing, H. and I are still well and safe. On the 29th I had two more combats, at Unao and Busserut Gunge, in which God gave me the victory, and I captured nineteen guns. Lieutenant Seton, who was acting as my aide-de-camp, was shot through the face, and his under jaw fractured. You do not know the lad, but may feel for him. . . . . What a mercy you did not come out to India! Pray for me and trust in God."

General Havelock had a noble coadjutor in General Neill. Most men would have expressed disappointment at the transfer of the chief command to another—specially when it had been confessedly well-fulfilled by himself; but Neill was a man above minor and personal considerations. He had reached Cawnpore on the 20th of July, and, after assisting in the passage of the Ganges by the army, had organised a police from the lowest caste of the population. By their means a large portion of the property stolen from Europeans at Cawnpore had been recovered; and many of the mutinous sepoys concerned in its cruel massacres were captured and executed. He had also formed an entrenched camp on the high ground on the river side, and had taken every precaution against a recurrence of the fearful tragedy of Cawnpore.

Along with the care of the sick and wounded, which increased his own difficulties, he received a request from General Havelock that he would send all the reinforcements in his power. Trusting to his own *prestige* and to the convalescents to hold the entrenchments, he at once sent every available soldier in Cawnpore to join the General at Mungulwar. It was the general impression that a nobler act was never performed.

These reinforcements had no sooner reached the camp than it was found that treachery had been at work. Writing on the 4th, Havelock says:—

"I was joined this morning by the half of Major Olpherts' battery, under Lieutenant Smithett. I inquired of him minutely how his detachment had behaved. He told me that the conduct of all had been very good, except his gun-lascars. They had, in April last, threatened to spike the guns whenever they might be engaged with the enemy. At Benares, Major Olpherts informed me that they had conducted themselves ill on the night of the mutiny.

"So far as depends on me, I cannot afford to have a single traitor in my camp. I paraded the detachment, and spoke to them all, both British and natives. I congratulated the former on having come into a camp of heroic soldiers, who had six times met the enemy, and every time defeated him and captured his cannon. The Lascars at this moment were facing the detachment; I turned to them, and told them what miscreants I had this morning discovered them to be—traitors in heart to their fostering Government. I made the British soldiers disarm them, and ordered them out of the camp under a light escort, to be employed under General Neill, in the labours of the entrenchment. He will look after them. If they attempt to desert, I have ordered them to be punished with death; the same if they refuse to work with the other soldiers. They shall do no other duty till I am better instructed.

"I have given the same orders regarding a detachment of sepoys of the 60th regiment, now on duty at Cawnpore."

The reinforcements, so generously sent by Neill, brought up General Havelock's force to 1400 men, with which he commenced, on the 4th of August, his second march to relieve Lucknow. He reached Unao on the following day, and found that place unoccupied; but the enemy were in force on their old ground at Busserut Gunge. Pressing forward with his volunteer cavalry, the General decided, on reconnoitring the position, to turn its left with Captain Maude's battery, the Highlanders and Sikhs under Colonel Hamilton. The attack was successful. The enemy abandoned their ground in confusion, suffering from the fire of the battery as they retreated on their second position, or rather on the town itself. They were here in great force, and their defences well planned. As the ground on either side of the road was little better than a lake, it was impossible to turn them, and Havelock advanced at the head of his infantry to drive them from the position. A vigorous fire was maintained for a short time against him, but he gained the town, drove the rebels through and out of it once more; and, crowding them in masses on the narrow bridge and causeway already described, inflicted upon them severe loss. The want of cavalry seriously neutralised this, as it had all the previous victories. The only guns taken were two, which had been placed upon the walls. The enemy had others in the field, but they were quickly removed. His loss was estimated by General Havelock at 300 killed and wounded. His own loss was two killed and twenty-three wounded. In the flight by the narrow bridge and road, it is probable that more of the enemy were lost than he states, for his despatches, with characteristic truthfulness and modesty, invariably present the lowest estimate of the achievements he effected and the dangers encountered by his forces.

But he must now again face an enemy he could not conquer. Cholera once more appeared to arrest his march. That invisible foe assailed his force severely on that evening of victory. He was encumbered with many cholera-stricken and dying men, whom he was bound, if possible, to save. Where could he seek safety from this assault? It could not be found among the swamps of Unao or Busserut Gunge, where the unburied bodies of many men and horses lay in the shallow and seething water. Baffled in his chief purpose, he had still the consolation that he did not retreat from the face of man, but before the pestilence. The next morning he fell back again on Mungulwar, a position sufficiently elevated to post his troops above the influence of the decimating miasma of the plain.

Several days were passed there for rest and refreshment; and during that period it became manifest to General Havelock that his present force was inadequate for the relief of Lucknow. He wrote:—

"CAMP, MUNGULWAR, *August* 6, 1857.

"I must prepare your Excellency for my abandonment, with great grief and reluctance, of the hope of relieving Lucknow. The only three staff-officers in my force whom I ever consult confidentially, but in whom I entirely confide, are unanimously of opinion that an advance to the walls of Lucknow involves the loss of this force. In this I concur. The only military question that remains, therefore, is whether that or the unaided destruction of the British garrison at Lucknow would be the greatest calamity to the State at this crisis. The loss of this force in a fruitless attempt to relieve Colonel Inglis, would, of course, involve his fall. I will remain, however, till the latest moment in this position, strengthening it, and hourly improving my bridge-communication with Cawnpore, in the hope that some error of the enemy may enable me to strike a blow against them, and give the garrison an opportunity of blowing up their works and cutting their way out.

"The enemy is in such force at Lucknow that to encounter him five marches from their position would be to court annihilation."

He was painfully conscious of the emergencies of

his position, and the following brief but solemn words addressed to his wife, shew how fully he confronted the gravest alternative:—

"BIVOUAC NUGHERUDAR, IN OUDE, SIX MILES FROM CAWNPORE, *Sunday, Aug.* 9, 1857.

"I know not when I may have leisure to write a line to you again, so I will avail myself, not of a Sabbath's rest, for that I have not, but of an incidental cessation of work, to give you my views. I have fought seven severe fights with the enemy, and by God's blessing have beat him in every one of them. . . . . But I will say no more of public matters than that I have everywhere beaten my foes, but that things are in a most perilous state. If we succeed in restoring anything it will be by God's especial and extraordinary mercy. H. is safe and well. He is my Deputy-Assistant-Adjutant-General, and my right arm. . . . . I must now write as one whom you may see no more, for the chances of war are heavy at this crisis. . . . . Thank God for my hope in the Saviour. We shall meet in heaven."

Having learned that a large force of the enemy had again assembled at Unao, with the intention of attacking his position at Mungulwar, or crushing part of his army, should he determine to recross the Ganges, he determined to seek them out on his old battle-field, rather than wait for them where he was. He had not now more than a thousand men, but they marched over the old ground again in excellent spirits on the morning of the 11th of August. The volunteer cavalry, few in number, but with all the daring spirit that actuated them of old, led the way. They were followed by the artillery, now formidable, from the number of their guns, supported by that matchless infantry which had never failed in any enterprise. The town of Unao was again reached, and the advanced picquets of the foe were pushed rapidly through its familiar streets. Having no tents, the men at nightfall bivouacked under some trees. They had no supplies, and many of them lay down to rest on the bare ground, without having tasted food that day. With the night came the rain, from which there was no shelter. As the sun rose next morning over the flooded plains they marched wet and weary to meet the rebel force.

The General anticipated that the enemy would not again venture to fight him with a narrow causeway and swamp in his rear. He was right. He found them drawn up at the village of Boorseake Chowki, nearer to Unao than Busherat. They had entrenched the village, which formed, probably, the centre of their line, and their guns were placed in good positions, among the gardens of the villagers. Their line is said by some accounts to have stretched over five miles; and their numbers have been estimated at 20,000, but the General gives a much lower number.

Havelock saw at a glance that this was not a case

for manœuvring; and great as the odds were, as the field must be won, it could only be by the force of sheer British valour. "Covered by artillery and skirmishers, our troops advanced in echelon of battalions from the right. As they came within range the enemy unmasked his batteries and poured in a deadly fire; round shot, shell, canister, grape, and shrapnel flew around, about, and amongst our men; fortunately the guns were levelled too high, and the round shot principally went over the heads of our advancing array. Still the fire was fearful; it did not, however, for an instant check our men; on they went covered by the guns, till at length these latter had obtained a sufficiently advanced position to get a flanking fire on the enemy's line. This appeared to paralyse them, and at the same moment the Highlanders, who were on the extreme right, making a dashing charge, carried the enemy's left battery of two guns. This completed their panic; they at once turned and fled, and our guns and their own captured batteries turning on them, completed their confusion. On the left we had been equally successful. There the enemy's cavalry had attempted to turn our flank; but the Madras Fusiliers nobly repulsed them: they fled with the remainder of the line.

The victory was gained; but it was one of those victories which must have called to the General's mind the despairing exclamation of Pyrrhus. He had lost one hundred and forty men out of a thousand, and had not advanced ten miles on his road to Lucknow. There was but one course to pursue,—to abandon all thought of reaching that place for the present, and to fall back upon Cawnpore. If there had been wanting any further argument to persuade him to this measure, he had it in the intelligence which reached him about this time, that the Nana Sahib had crossed in great force, and was threatening that station.

"His mind was made up. But he held possession of the field of battle, rested on it for two hours, then, taking with him the two guns, trophies of the victory, slowly retired on Mungulwar. The following morning, the 13th August, he recrossed the Ganges, and rejoined General Neill at Cawnpore." *

He arrived only just in time. Nana Sahib had collected a numerous body at Bithoor, and was threatening Cawnpore from all directions. His cavalry had even penetrated into the suburbs of the town. The communications with Allahabad were in danger, or by that date absolutely stopped; a difficulty foreseen by General Havelock before his advance through Unao and his battle of the 12th of August. Nothing was done on the 14th, for the effective men needed rest, and care was required for the sick and the wounded. To reopen the communication with Allahabad, on the 15th, General Neill marched out of the entrenchments at the head of a considerable force in the direction of the Pandoo

* "Mutiny of the Bengal Army."

Nuddee. He encountered the enemy in one of their favourite positions for intercepting reinforcements, and gained an easy victory over them. Unable to withstand the vigour of his first volley, they fled almost without resistance.

On the return of Neill, Havelock determined to march against Bithoor next day. About noon he came in sight of the enemy, consisting of the 31st and 42d mutinied sepoys from Saugor, the 17th from Fyzabad, squadrons of the 2d Light Cavalry and 3d Irregulars, detachments from several infantry regiments of sepoys, and part of Nana Sahib's retainers; altogether numbering 4000 men, and very strongly posted. The plain before their position was covered with thick jungle and sugar canes, which reached high above the heads of the men, while the batteries, effectually masked, were defended by thick ramparts flanked by entrenched quadrangles. The position was also flanked by villages, and comprehended the town of Bithoor, a place of some magnitude.

"On observing the enemy's position, and their infantry drawn up in front of it, Havelock brought his guns to the front, and opened upon them; but it soon appeared that this was only a part of their plan to draw us on, for no sooner had our guns opened than the enemy retreated into their defences, and their guns at the same moment poured in a tremendous shower of shot and shell on our advancing line. During the twenty minutes that this was kept up our men lay down, replying with their rifles, whilst our artillery also were blazing at the foe. But at the end of that time, finding that our guns made little impression, and did not even silence their fire, although within six hundred yards of their position, Havelock resolved to have resort to the bayonet. A simultaneous advance was made in skirmishing order on the entrenched quadrangles before alluded to. These were quickly cleared, the sepoys retreating to the two villages in the rear. Whilst the Madras Fusiliers went in pursuit of these, the 78th Highlanders advanced on the battery, alternately lying down and moving on, as it vomited forth or ceased its fierce discharges of grape and canister. The rebels, confident in their position, awaited the approach of our men; but no sooner had the foremost of them cleared the parapet than the sepoys' hearts failed them, and they fled in confusion. Their position was so strong, and our men were so exhausted by the heat of the sun and by their own exertions, that a determined stand here might have changed the fortunes of the day. No fact, however, has been more clearly established in the course of this insurrection than that Asiatics, whatever may be their strength, cannot resist the charge of the smallest number of Englishmen. There is something in the sight of Europeans advancing at a run, with stern visage, bayonets fixed, determination marked in every movement of the body, which appals them; they cannot stand it—they never have stood it yet.

"Meanwhile, the Fusiliers, pursuing the enemy out of the entrenched quadrangles, came down upon the loopholed villages in the rear. Not an instant did they pause, but, rushing into them, gained them with scarce a struggle,—the enemy being quite unable to make head against their impetuosity. In the rear of these villages was a little bridge leading to the town: across this the Fusiliers, now joined by the whole force, drove them, a few only endeavouring to make a fruitless stand; these were overcome; the remainder fled, followed by our men right through the town. Further it was impossible to pursue them. Our troops, exposed to a hot sun, and undergoing fearful exertions, were completely knocked up. They bivouacked on the ground which they had won, and the next morning returned to Cawnpore, to take up a commanding position on the plain of Subada, close to the spot on which our heroic garrison had so long defended themselves." *

That morning Havelock issued the following field-force order:—

"The Brigadier-General commanding congratulates the troops on the result of their exertions in the combat of yesterday. The enemy were driven, with the loss of 250 killed and wounded, from one of the strongest positions in India, which they obdurately defended. They were the flower of the mutinous soldiery, flushed with the successful defection at Saugor and Fyzabad: yet they stood only one short hour against a handful of soldiers of the

* "Mutiny of the Bengal Army."

State, whose ranks had been thinned by sickness and the sword.

"May the hopes of treachery and rebellion be ever thus blasted; and, if conquest can now be achieved under the most trying circumstances, what will be the triumph and retribution of the time when the armies from China, from the Cape, and from England, shall sweep through the land? Soldiers! in that moment your labours, your privations, your sufferings, and your valour will not be forgotten by a grateful country. You will be acknowledged to have been the stay and prop of British India in the time of her severest trial."

"With this action," we quote again from the "Mutiny of the Bengal Army," "terminated Havelock's first grand campaign for the relief of Lucknow. Strictly speaking, perhaps, it was concluded on the day on which he recrossed the Ganges. In this great effort he had fought five pitched battles against an enemy vastly superior in numbers; he had been compelled to leave open his communications, to carry with him sick and wounded, to dare the rays of a scorching, often a deadly sun, to march without tents, to carry with him every article of supply. With these difficulties to encounter, he had advanced three times, and three times had struck so great a terror into the enemy that his retreat had been invariably unmolested. He found, indeed, that he could gain victories, but that, for want of cavalry, he could not follow them up; that the enormous numbers of the enemy enabled them to recruit, and more than recruit, their losses as he advanced; that another large body, under the Nana Sahib and Jussa Singh, was always ready to interpose between him and the Ganges. He fought, in fact, more conscious that victory would secure his retreat, than facilitate an advance, which, with his numbers, was impossible."

The army of deliverance was now doomed to a short period of enforced repose. The troops needed rest to prepare for the terrible struggle then in store for them. They had not raised the siege of Lucknow, but they had indirectly relieved the garrison of the Residency there, for by their successes and their threatening attitude they compelled the besiegers to weaken their force, and allowed the besieged an opportunity, which they adopted, of adding to their stores by successful sallies from their shattered stronghold, and of repairing their dilapidated defences.

In the correspondence kept up with Bonna few terse sentences sufficed for a most suggestive description of this most serious crisis. Letters from home, it will be seen, were as cold water to a thirsty soul. Nor, in this confidential despatch of the undemonstrative warrior, will the reader fail to remark his sympathy for the hardships and sufferings of the private soldier:—

"CAMP, CAWNPORE, *August* 27, 1857.

"It is an age since I have had a letter from any

of you. None I think since I left Calcutta. Here I am in the midst of most exciting affairs, which hardly give me breathing time, but I snatch half an hour to tell you that by God's blessing H. and I are still alive and well. We have fought nine fights with the enemy, everywhere defeated him, and captured forty-two pieces of cannon. Sir Henry Lawrence, the most amiable of men, was badly wounded on the 2d July, and died on the 4th. . . . Troops are coming up to me, but I fear that it will be too late, and that the place will fall before I can re-enter Oude. . . . This campaigning in the rain is trying work. Cholera carries off my brave British troops, and it is only here that I have been able to give them a little repose from the most harassing duties and operations. . . . I have had for two months the power of life and death in my hands, for all the provinces are under martial law. I trust God has enabled me to use it discreetly. J. is at Peshawur, where all is tranquil. Of course we never get a line from him, for all the communications above this are interrupted. Love to the dear children."

"CAMP, CAWNPORE, *Aug.* 30, 1857.

"I have this morning got your letter of the 21st June, *viâ* Marseilles. . . . . My reinforcements are coming in, and, by God's blessing, I shall soon be at the fellows again. . . . . Thank George for his ten-year-old letter. . . . . Love to the children."

To the Rev. B. Lewis, Calcutta, he wrote, in reply to a letter of Christian sympathy :—

"I am thankful to you and to all my good friends in Calcutta for their intercession at a throne of grace and mercy on my behalf. No disaster, great or small, has befallen me or my troops. By the blessing of God I have defeated our enemies in nine successive actions, and captured forty-eight of their cannon with no great loss on my part. But my force is small, and has been dreadfully thinned by cholera and other diseases incident to British soldiers exposed, often without tents, to the inclemency of this season. I have been compelled, therefore, to await reinforcements, which are coming up to me, before again advancing to Lucknow, where I yet hope to relieve its gallant and much-enduring garrison. It is commanded by Colonel Inglis, a man of piety, I believe. Let him share your prayers. I set up no pretensions to military skill, but I have endeavoured to conduct my operations on the principles which soldiers recognise as sound; and thus far God has blessed my endeavours.

"H. HAVELOCK."

Never was Havelock's trust in God more necessary or more available than now. Impressed every day more deeply with the righteousness of the determination to put down this terrible rebellion, he might well have doubted of success had he walked by sight. "Where is now your God?" might have been the triumphant taunt of Nana Sahib, as he had to turn his back on the sufferers at Lucknow, and to go with his own suffering comrades into Cawnpore again, with that well to remind them of what was daily hanging over their own heads.

"Our God is in the heavens," was the veteran's unfaltering reply to all scorners; and then in the multitude of his thoughts within him, he remembered that everlasting covenant which is ordered in all things and sure, and those promises which are in every jot and tittle of them yea and amen in Jesus Christ. To the full assurance of his faith there came to him in this time of his heaviest trial the commandment not to be afraid, only to believe. His first hour of devotional retirement on getting back into Cawnpore found him very much in Abraham's position, who staggered not at the promise of God through unbelief, but was strong in faith, giving glory to God,—being fully persuaded that what He had promised He was able also to perform. Luther's hymn was the thing for him—

> "Put thou thy trust in God,
> In duty's path go on;
> Fix on His Word thy steadfast eye,
> So shall thy work be done."

With the responsibilities pressing upon him he was vigorously at his post. His religion kept him alike from foolhardiness and despair.

CHAPTER XIV.

THE MARCH TO THE ALUM BAGH.

On General Outram's arrival in Calcutta, he had almost immediately been appointed to the military command of the Cawnpore and Dinapore stations. It was under his judicious arrangements that the annexation of Oude had been effected. No other officer in the service was better acquainted with that kingdom than he; and the decision of the Government, in now again placing him in that important command, was generally approved.

Havelock had served under Outram in the Persian war, and had won his high esteem. Long, indeed, before that campaign—even when they were engaged in hostilities in Affghanistan and the Punjaub—his professional and personal worth was well understood. No man, therefore, could appreciate better the splendid struggle that Havelock had conducted from Futtehpore to Busserut Gunge than his former companion-in-arms. Every rood of the road was accurately mapped on his mind, and all the resources of the enemy had been calculated carefully, and were thoroughly known by him.

Early in September, General Outram arrived at Allahabad with the reinforcements destined for the relief of Lucknow. They were small, but the exigency was most urgent. Informed of their advance, hope reassumed the ascendant, and Havelock made preparations for employing them to the best advantage. He had informed himself thoroughly of the surpassing difficulties of his enterprise. The inadequacy of his force was his great cause for apprehension. Of this he complained incessantly. His men were brave enough for anything, but, in proportion to the service required, they were miserably few.

Nor must it be forgotten that, in addition to every heroic impulse, he had cause for strong personal anxiety; and, if anything could have converted into nervous precipitancy his sublime and calculating courage, it would have been the thought of beloved kindred suffering all the miseries to which the Residency was now exposed.

"CAMP, CAWNPORE, *Sept.* 12, 1857.

"Our latest safe day from this is the 16th; but on the 15th I expect my reinforcements, which Sir J. Outram accompanies, and then will commence war's hurry-skurry again. . . . . I have a most arduous task before me in endeavouring, with not very adequate means, to relieve Lucknow. I will do my best; but the operation is most delicate, and there is too great a probability of the Residency falling into the hands of the foe before we can relieve it. The wretches will put every one to the sword, and the poor girl Mary and her husband are shut up in the place."

On the 15th, the 5th Fusiliers, part of the 90th Light Infantry, and some companies of the 78th came into Cawnpore, and the next day brought General Outram. The month had not been lost. Sick men were strong again, and the wounded had recovered and were well. The entrenchments of Cawnpore were completed, and the bridge of boats had been put in order.

Arrived at Cawnpore, General Outram was entitled, in virtue of his superior rank, to assume the command; but knowing how dear to Havelock was the object on which he was bent, and to effect which he had already made one most noble though unsuccessful effort, with a magnanimity as rare as it was generous, he waived his rank, and left his old companion-in-arms in the chief command.

"The important duty of first relieving Lucknow," said he in his Divisional Order of the night of the 16th, "has been intrusted to Major-General Havelock, C.B., and Major-General Outram feels that it is due to this distinguished officer, and the strenuous and noble exertions which he has already made to effect that object, that to him should accrue the honour of the achievement.

"Major-General Outram is confident that the

great end for which General Havelock and his brave troops have so long and so gloriously fought will now, under the blessing of Providence, be accomplished.

"The Major-General, therefore, in gratitude for, and admiration of, the brilliant deeds in arms achieved by General Havelock and his gallant troops, will cheerfully waive his rank on the occasion, and will accompany the force to Lucknow in his civil capacity as Chief Commissioner of Oude, tendering his military services to General Havelock as a volunteer.

"On the relief of Lucknow, the Major-General will resume his position at the head of the forces."

In acknowledgment of this generous action, the following Order was issued on the same evening by General Havelock:—

"Brigadier-General Havelock, in making known to the column the kind and generous determination of General Sir James Outram, K.C.B., to leave to him the task of relieving Lucknow and rescuing its gallant and enduring garrison, has only to express his hope that the troops will strive, by their exemplary and gallant conduct in the field, to justify the confidence thus reposed in them."

Leaving Cawnpore, now in a state of defence, in charge of Colonel O'Brien, Havelock crossed the Ganges on the 19th. This was an arduous affair, for the river, then in flood, was running rapidly, and there were heavy guns, elephants, camels, ammunition waggons, and commissariat stores, as well as long trains of armed men, doolies for the wounded, and troops of burden-bearing coolies to be got over. At length it was effected, and the march began.

On the previous night, most of the troops had been marched down to the river's bank to await the advance of the morrow. As they moved along, the regimental colours carried in their dark cloth covering, rose up now and again from the forest of glistening bayonets, "like yew trees in a garden." The moon struggled through the rain which had been falling all the day, and threw a dim light over the river, looming mournfully on the blackened ruin where the brave old soldier, Sir H. Wheeler, and his devoted garrison, had closed their last days on earth.

The army was divided into two brigades of infantry—the first comprising the 5th Fusiliers, the 84th Queen's, part of the 64th Foot, and the 1st Madras Fusiliers; General Neill in command: the second brigade was formed by the 78th, the 90th, and the Sikh Regiment of Ferozepore; Brigadier Hamilton, of the 78th, in command. The third brigade was artillery, and consisted of Captain Maude's, Captain Olphert's, and Brevet-Major Eyre's batteries, under the command of Major Cope. The cavalry were the small body of volunteers often mentioned and a few Irregular horsemen of a native corps, with captain Barrow in command. A small body of Engineers, under Captain Crommelin, was attached.

After some skirmishing by the river's banks had cleared away the enemy, the army advanced by most fatiguing marches, for the Ganges having acquired its extreme height, had overflowed its banks for several miles on the Oude side. The water, as in nearly all similar cases, though still, was in some places deep upon the fields, and the sun was beating fiercely on the men. Very few tents had been taken with them, and provisions for only fifteen days had been brought over. The force was not, therefore, needlessly encumbered with stores; but they had a large park of artillery and an abundant supply of ammunition.

As Havelock advanced the rebels rapidly retreated, and then of him and his force nothing was heard at Cawnpore for many days. "Since the day that the tail of our army left," says a correspondent of the *Hurkaru*, "no vestige of news has reached us. They ploughed a way through the tide of rebellion which overflows Oude; but the waves closed again, and we have no means of hearing from them or of communicating with them. Yesterday a hundred men, who had been sent to keep the Lucknow road open, were cut up by the rebels almost to a man, and our cossids have returned with 'no news.'"

Another correspondent wrote:—"It seems that many cossids (messengers) have been despatched from General Havelock's camp, but the enemy have kept up such a strict blockade in the rear of his force that to pass was impossible."

It was Saturday afternoon. The labour of crossing the guns had been very severe, and the army was halted for the night among the sand-hills on the edge of the river, which was now raised above two miles from its ordinary channels.

The next was the day of rest; and except that the volunteer cavalry went out to reconnoitre, the army was permitted to repose. Many great battles have been fought on that day; but General Havelock in his own practice avoided fighting on the Sabbath whenever he could. He had seen nothing in this case to be gained by a departure from his usual rule, and he probably gained much by its observance. He knew that many of his men had already advanced rapidly from Allahabad to Cawnpore, and he wanted them to move still more rapidly on towards Lucknow. He had more heavy guns to bring over, and the delay permitted him to bring up more baggage. Although, therefore, the enemy was entrenched in force two miles from his position, and had fired on the volunteer cavalry, he permitted them to remain unmolested.

The weather changed again that afternoon. The hot sun was hidden and shrouded in thick clouds, and the rain fell in torrents upon the almost unsheltered army. Through the entire night it came down in sheets, and the soldier's miserable bivouac was turned into an immense puddle. Men slept, and from their fatigue slept soundly, until called by the bugle with the dawn of Monday morning. Shortly after daybreak the column was again in motion. They had not advanced more than a mile before the artillery of the foe opened upon them. Major Eyre's battery was ordered to the front, and answered the fire. General Havelock had, moreover, no intention of walking his men straight up to the batteries which his opponents had taken days, or perhaps weeks, to prepare and strengthen. He ordered the artillery, protected by the 5th, to throw shot and shell among them for a time, until he had moved through the swamps a strong force on their right. The close practice of his formidable guns soon began to tell fearfully upon the rebels, while the ponderous shells, cast among their numerous cavalry with the precision of rifle practice, carried confusion into their ranks. The enemy detached a horse battery to attack Havelock's flank. They were outmanœuvred, however; and long ere it had reached its intended position Captain Maude was seen spurring in hot haste across the field, at the head of his horse artillery. Round after round was rapidly exchanged, and in less than a quarter of an hour the guns of the enemy were silenced. By this time the infantry had turned their right, and this completed their defeat. Their guns were horsed rapidly, and their positions quickly abandoned. Two of their guns were left for our infantry. They did not wait to meet the bayonets which were closing fast with them. But as they fled they encountered a new foe. Sir James Outram, heading the volunteer cavalry, turned their flight into a rout, capturing two more guns, and leaving 120 of the enemy sabred on the plain. This battle of Mungulwar caused little loss to General Havelock's army, but it was attended by serious results to his enemy, who fought no more until they reached the Alum Bagh.

The rebels had made admirable arrangements to receive General Havelock, should he advance in the direction that they expected him to take. He would have had to storm a breastwork so formidable that it had afterwards to be levelled before his baggage-waggons and guns could pass. He selected another path, and for that departure from the high road the enemy were not prepared.

The battle over, the march followed—a long and dreary march amidst a deluge. The rain had poured incessantly upon a country which was already turned into a lake, and in many places, as the army moved on, the water was of great depth. Passing Unao, the scene of former conflicts, through Busserut Gunge,—all abandoned by the enemy in their flight,—Havelock's force marched that day twenty miles in an Indian flood, after gaining their decisive victory. Towards evening they reached an abandoned village, cheerless and dirty, but still capable of affording the shelter which all required, and here they passed the night.

Early in the morning of the 22d the army continued its march, the rain still falling heavily. Many of the coolies who had been engaged to assist in the conveyance of the baggage and the wounded, had deserted during the night, for they dreaded the approach to Lucknow. But there was no time to wait to supply their loss. Precious lives were being hourly sacrificed in that beleaguered station, and to its inmates every day was an age. Onward Havelock and his noble army pressed, beset with difficulty, but sustained by the hope of effecting the object of their march. The day's advance was an incessant struggle through fields now turned into morasses and swamps by the ceaseless rain, with heavy guns and lumbering waggons, delayed by some accident or some new obstruction at almost every turn.

After a toilsome march of fourteen miles through a lane or stream of mud, the force reached another deserted village, and in its empty houses they found a shelter for another comfortless night. The artillery booming around the Residency of Lucknow were now heard; and a royal salute from their heavy guns was fired, in the hope that their friends in danger might hear the report, and comprehend its purpose.

The 23d opened with little change in the dull leaden sky. Noon had passed and they had not yet reached Lucknow, while their cavalry, then in advance, had brought no intelligence of the enemy. At length, at two o'clock, they were seen slowly falling back. This excited apprehension, and immediately afterwards, as the force advanced, the rebel army was discovered in great force, their right drawn up behind a chain of hillocks, and their left resting on the enclosure of the Alum Bagh. Havelock now perceived that he was not to enter Lucknow without a desperate struggle. A single glance convinced him that the flower of the enemy was before him, and that here the first passage to the Residency must be fought. He made his dispositions with that alacrity and precision which had so often been the means of baffling his foes; and, although his troops had marched with little intermission for seven hours, no time was lost in attempting to clear the road to Lucknow.

The mutineers had selected their position with the view of neutralising Havelock's habit of turning the lines of his opponents, of which they had obtained experience in frequent and disastrous engagements. The trunk-road passed through deep and wide morasses, which, at that season, ran close up to its edges, and were altogether impassable. Immediately where the morasses ceased, and firmer footing could be obtained, and on a rising ground, the rebel army were massed in strong battalions of infantry, with many guns, and cavalry on the centre, the left, and the right. The only available means of attack was by this road; and upon it the enemy converged the fire of their artillery. Havelock's guns replied with some effect; but he instantly saw that his men were too closely grouped. His infantry were, therefore, pushed forward rapidly upon his old plan; and, although a hurricane of round shot and shell were ploughing through their ranks, and thinning their sections, they never faltered. At length his left enveloped the enemy's right; and charging through the soft ground, where the men sank ankle-deep at every step, they drove their foe before them, capturing one village after another, and ultimately seizing five guns.

While the enemy's right was thus crushed and driven from the field, his centre was exposed to the effective artillery fire from Havelock's batteries; and as the battle now pressed upon his left, that wing and the centre at length broke up and fled, Sir James Outram, at the head of his handful of cavalry, bravely pursuing the enemy, regardless of the odds; till after a tedious, but never dubious fight, the battle of the Alum Bagh was won.

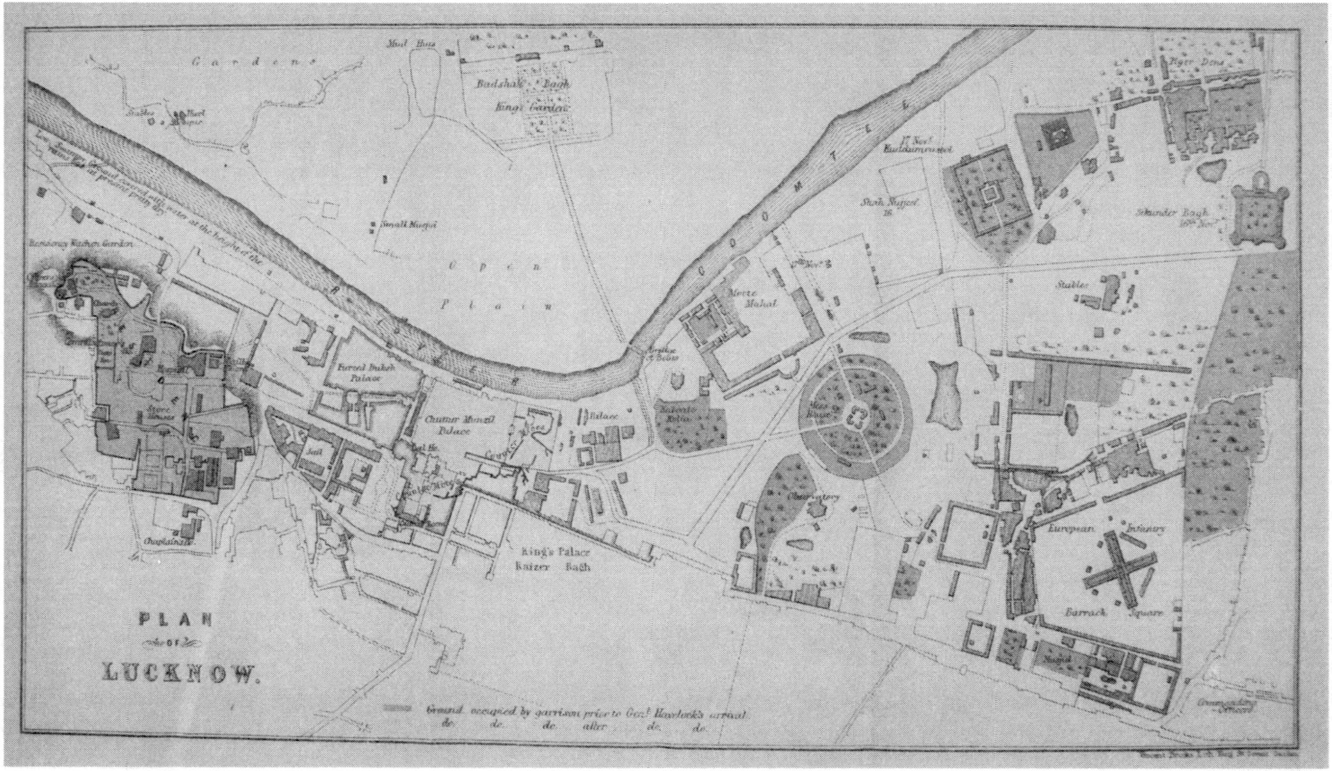
PLAN
OF
LUCKNOW.
Gardens
Badshah Bagh
King's Garden
Small Musjid
Open Plain
River Goomtee
Motee Mahal
Furreed Buksh Palace
Chuttur Munzil Palace
Jail
Palace
King's Palace
Kaizer Bagh
Observatory
Secunder Bagh
Stables
Shah Nujjef
European Infantry
Barrack Square
Ground occupied by garrison prior to Genl. Havelock's arrival.
do. do. do. after do. do.

CHAPTER XV.

THE SIEGE OF THE RESIDENCY.

THE death of Sir Henry Lawrence had been a grievous blow. On his judgment, wisdom, and cool determination the garrison could unhesitatingly lean, and in his Christian character they recognised an element of unspeakable comfort in a contest which was about, they knew, to become a struggle for precious life. And when, on the 4th of July, he died, all ranks felt that there had passed away from among them one whose foresight, wisdom, and fertility of resource had deserved the confidence they had always placed in him, and whose Christian urbanity had made him a public benefactor, and to each of them a warm personal friend. When he found his end was near, Lawrence bequeathed to Major Banks his civil appointment, and to Brigadier Inglis the chief military command, with his invaluable legacy—his advice and counsel for the future conduct of the defence. Not long was Major Banks to fill this important office; for, while examining a critical outpost on the top of Mr Gubbins' house, a few days afterwards, he was struck by a shot in the head and killed.

The line of defence had been formed by Sir Henry Lawrence and his brave associates with consummate skill.* It consisted of a ditch and parapet, at the edge of which the ground begins to descend, and a long space of high ground was taken advantage of to construct a battery, named the Redan. The ditch and parapet nearly encircled the Treasury, and ended at the Baillie Guard gate, near Dr Fayrer's house. From this up to the Thuggee Gaol the defence consisted of the compound walls, with ditch and palisade inside, and barricades across the lanes which separated the compounds. The left corner of the Thuggee Gaol was on the prolongation of the Cawnpore road. Here, therefore, a battery was constructed, merely to sweep that road, its position not enabling it to be put to any other use, and the supposition being that one great source of danger was the advance and attack of troops from Cawnpore. The walls of the Thuggee Gaol and the natives' houses, with stockading in front, were the line of defence there; a parapet and ditch and the walls of out-houses encircled Mr Gubbins' compound. The walls of the Residency out-houses were, again, the defence there; thence a parapet following the edge of the high ground formed the boundary up to Lieut.

* We are indebted for the substance of the following narrative to Lieutenant Innes, of the Bengal Engineers, one of the garrison.

Innes' house; from which point a deep ditch to the Redan completed the line of defence. Most of the houses bordering close on the entrenchments had been levelled, except those on the Cawnpore battery side, but a few that would probably serve to traverse the former from artillery had been left standing. These and every building within musketry range became filled with the enemy's sharpshooters, who were able, specially with the 8-inch howitzer taken some time before at Chinnahut, to keep up a most mischievous and deadly fire.

After the first week the musketry fire got less deadly, both from its not being so briskly kept up, and also from the troops having got more cognisant of the localities to be avoided, and more cautious as to how they exposed themselves. Still the loss averaged about ten daily. To put a stop to this, the parapets forming the entrenchments were raised, trenches excavated deeper, and roads defiladed as much as possible. As the enemy's fire got less mischievous, and the ammunition and provisions were known to be amply sufficient for a much longer time than the siege was expected to last, the garrison began to regain heart. On the first rumours of the reverse at Chinnahut, related at page 162, all the labourers and prisoners employed at the works had rushed off in a body with nearly all the tools and implements. What the garrison chiefly suffered from was, the want of these men and materials, the absconding of servants, the continuance of rain, and the necessity for incessant work either with the musket or the spade. Another source of much depression was the total absence of communication with the outer world. Up to the arrival of Havelock's and Outram's reinforcements, a period of nearly three months from the commencement of the siege, only three letters reached the garrison.

Rumours of mining, on the part of the enemy, also began to be circulated, but no sounds could be heard, and it was therefore decided that vigilance in listening for indications of mining was all that could be attempted; that taking the initiative in mining would be teaching the enemy a lesson, at which they would probably be but too apt scholars, and in which they would be able to check and overpower the garrison completely from their command of labour alone. Among the most important precautions against any open assault of the enemy was the establishment of one look-out from the top of the Post-office, and another from the lower part of the Residency. The garrison were thus able to watch and record any movements of the enemy in larger bodies than usual, or in unwonted directions.

On the morning of the 20th July they were noticed to be assembling and moving in great numbers. The troops were all turned out, and at ten o'clock the enemy exploded a mine, which was evidently intended to injure the Redan, but which reached barely half way, and was therefore harmless. This explosion was the prelude to a most fierce assault—a furious fusillade, shot and shell flying in every direction. The only opposition the garrison made to this was to keep well under cover. At a few points, however, the enemy attempted to storm, as at the Cawnpore Battery, the Brigade Mess, Innes' House, and the Redan Battery; but the obstacles planted at those places fully answered their purpose, and they were checked in their advance, with severe loss. Thus obliged to retire, and the point where they were most thickly congregated being discovered, they were so well shelled, especially by Lieutenants Bonham and M'Farlane, that numbers were killed, and by four o'clock in the afternoon their fusillade had almost entirely ceased. Spies reported the enemy's loss to amount to between 800 and 1000 men. On our side, so steadily had the men behaved, that only three were killed and seven wounded.

After the failure of this first attempt to storm the entrenchment, the garrison suffered much less annoyance from the musketry. But the foe began to bring more guns into the field, and also became more expert cannoniers. Shot, shell, and carcases invaded the Residency, so that the upper storeys had to be evacuated. The rumours of mining also increased, and as the enemy had taken the initiative, Captain Fulton organised a body of miners, six of whom were Europeans and eighteen natives, and began a series of defensive mines. By attention and vigilance, the probable direction of some of the enemy's galleries were discovered, countermines were excavated, and by dint of patience, skill, courage, and judgment, Captain Fulton and Lieutenant Hutchinson got possession of and destroyed two of the enemy's galleries, directed at the Brigade Mess and the Cawnpore Battery. But they had been constructing a third mine, which was exploded under the outer wall of the Sikh Cavalry Lines, burying seven drummers in its ruins. The stamping of the horses' feet had probably prevented the sounds of the excavation from being heard. This was the solitary instance in which the enemy succeeded in their efforts underground. Its result was a large breach; but so cowardly were they that they made no attempt to storm it. It was quickly barricaded, and the day which had so unhappy a commencement proved one of the most auspicious during the siege, for a party made a sortie under Captain Fulton and demolished the buildings in the neighbourhood of the shaft where the mine had begun.

"No conception can be formed," says an officer who was on the spot, "of the amount of work the engineers had to perform. The great success attending the operations, under such unparalleled difficulties, forms a new era in the history of countermining."

On the 24th July the first letter arrived which they had received since the commencement of the siege. It was from one of the officers in General Havelock's Staff, and announced the presence of his army on the Oude side of the Ganges, opposite Cawnpore, and the probability of the relief of Lucknow in two or three days. The joy of the beleaguered garrison on the receipt of this intelligence needs no description. A reply was immediately returned, begging that two rockets might be sent up the moment that the relief arrived at the outskirts of the city, in order that they might make what efforts they could to aid their comrades in the perilous passage to the Residency. It need not be told how many eyes were on the stretch for weary days and nights, anxious to be the first to announce to their fellow-prisoners the joyful news of succour at hand, nor how the long days passed and hearts grew sick with despair when the expected aid remained unheard and unseen. "We knew not then," says Brigadier Inglis, "nor did we learn till the 29th of August, or thirty-five days later, that the relieving force, after having fought most nobly to effect our deliverance, had been obliged to fall back for reinforcements; and this was the last communication we received until two days before the arrival of Sir James Outram on the 25th September."

To resume our narrative :—No further signs of mining having been heard, the besieged had ventured to hope that the destruction of the enemy's galleries had put a stop to his endeavours in this mode of warfare. But they were soon undeceived. On the 10th of August the same signs were seen from the top of the Post-office of the assemblage of troops which had been visible on the 20th July. As on that occasion, the assault began by the explosion of mines; one opposite Mr Sago's house formed a perfectly innocuous crater, and blew out chiefly at its own shaft. The other blew down the stockading outside the right of the Convalescent Hospital (formerly the Thuggee Gaol) and the left of the Brigade Mess, but it did no other harm. The assaults were less courageous and more easily repulsed. The fusillade was neither so lively nor so well kept up.

Two days after this attack, the enemy having commenced a fresh mine opposite Mr Sago's house, a sortie of a small party was organised to destroy the building where the shaft was situated; but, on sallying out, finding an overwhelming force ready for them, they retreated without loss, the officer and the leading files having surprised and shot down a few of the enemy. A countermine was the only resource left. One was prepared, undermining the enemy's building, and, exploding the charge where the enemy were known to be well crowded, it demolished the house and gallery, burying twenty-five or thirty of the foe in the ruins.

Towards the end of August a strong accession to the artillery force of the enemy was noticed; and they also chose the sites of their batteries with more judgment. One was planted so as to be certain of injuring either Lieutenant Innes' house, the church, the Residency, Dr Fayrer's house, or the Post-office.

And they also appeared to be becoming more systematic, or at any rate to have fixed on one decided point of attack, as they planted no fewer than seven guns against Mr Gubbins' house.

The cause of this became soon apparent. A second letter reached the garrison, brought in by Ungnoo, a pensioner, the same man who had succeeded in smuggling in the first. This was from General Havelock, informing them of his expectation of receiving reinforcements in the middle of September, and of the impossibility of his coming to them until then. This was a great damper to their hopes; but their provisions were amply sufficient; they despised their foe, and the style and tone of the letter gave its promises of relief a stamp of probability on which they might cheerfully rely. The Nana and his forces, they further heard, had been driven hopelessly from Cawnpore.

In the beginning of September the enemy, aware of Havelock's intentions, again began to take seriously to offensive measures. On the 3d a mine was discovered at work towards the Brigade Mess. Lieutenant Hutchinson countermined, and obliged them to stop it, at a distance of fifteen yards. On the same day, they mined towards Captain Saunders' post. Lieutenant Innes countermined and blew in their gallery, when their miners were still at work. Nothing daunted, they struck off a fresh branch next day, against the same post. This time the garrison excavated into the enemy's gallery, took possession of it, and, laying a train, destroyed the whole of their mine in that direction. The enemy having been observed to be strengthening their artillery opposite the Baillie Guard gate, Captain Fulton had constructed and armed a one-gun 18-pound battery near the Treasury on its left, and had manned it with faithful sepoys, under Lieutenant Aitken. The three operations, completing the Treasury Battery, the destruction of the mine at Captain Saunders', and the stoppage of that at the Brigade Mess, were all performed on the night of the 4th.

On the morning of the 5th the usual signs of an assault were seen. But the enemy soon learnt how their plans had been defeated. One mine they found a mass of rubbish; the other they knew to be far short of its aim, but they blew it up, probably, in spite; they opened fire on the Baillie Guard gate, only to find their guns silenced by the newly-constructed battery; they exploded a third mine towards Mr Gubbins' compound, but as usual the gallery was short, and it proved harmless; they sent some new arrivals to storm the Brigade Mess, only to have to retire, leaving, it was said, 100 of their comrades lying dead at the stockade.

During the siege the partial relief effected by the advance of Havelock's column was sensibly felt in the garrison, by the enemy's works being interrupted or suspended.

All the while that this fearful struggle was going

on, the patient endurance and Christian resignation of the ladies and soldiers' wives animated by their example the devoted band who defended them. Many of them had been made widows and their children had become fatherless, but they never ceased to exhibit in the common danger a self-devotion that renders the part they took in the defence of Lucknow indelibly memorable.

Danger at length became all but extreme, and some of the besieged despaired. Their provisions were failing fast. Disease in aggravated forms was amongst them, and death had made grievous inroads on their number. More than three hundred of the men had died, and many more had succumbed to cholera, small-pox, and fever. Nearly everything was getting to depend upon the continued faithfulness of the native soldiers. Hitherto they had remained loyal, notwithstanding the incessant efforts made by the enemy to undermine their loyalty. Should they prove unfaithful, as their countrymen had so often and so unexpectedly done elsewhere, then indeed might the garrison give up hope, for those fearful duties, imperatively imposed upon a force already thinned by death and weakened by disease, would too surely have laid the garrison at the feet of their ferocious enemies.

The heroism and skill of that illustrious defence have few parallels in history. With batteries that had not only been hastily constructed, but were surrounded by lofty buildings which afforded a safe shelter to at least eight thousand malignant and well-trained marksmen, thirsting like tigers for their prey; with large guns playing on them night and day; with scanty and indifferent food; with sickness in its worst and most distressing forms; with all the vicissitudes of heat, cold, and rain; with the harass of false alarms, that broke in most cruelly, every night, upon the brief interval of repose; with artillerymen so few that the gunners had to rush from one battery to another wherever the fire happened to be the hottest;—the maintenance of the position seemed to be impossible, and yet with all these difficulties within that Residency, its illustrious band of not five hundred men held its own against at least fifty thousand, without *losing a foot of ground or conceding to the enemy a solitary instance of success.*

Such was the condition of the garrison when the firing of the artillery at the action of Alum Bagh, on the 23d, which was plainly heard by them, announced the arrival of the army of relief within the suburbs of the city.

CHAPTER XVI.

THE RELIEF OF LUCKNOW.

THE city of Lucknow, with its narrow, tortuous streets, still lay between the beleaguered garrison and the army of relief, a wide plain intervening besides between the city and the Alum Bagh. The nearest way would have been over the plain and along the street, of which the Cawnpore road from the Alum Bagh is a continuation. This would have taken the force direct to the gates of the Residency; but the Generals knew that the enemy had anticipated their advance by that road, and had made vigorous preparations to receive them. Deep and broad trenches were cut, palisades intersected the streets at short intervals, while every other house had been extemporised into a garrison and filled with sepoys. To have taken the troops through such a fire would have been madness, and it was not long entertained.

The circuitous route by the Dilkoosha, Martiniere, and the Sikunder Bagh, was equally impracticable; for the long rain had turned the fields for the most part into a huge morass, through which the passage of heavy artillery and ammunition waggons, indispensable in such an expedition, would have been impossible; and that route was also abandoned. For similar reasons other roads were deemed equally impracticable, and the Generals determined to reach the Residency by the way subsequently adopted.

Early on the morning of the 25th the army was on the move. On the previous day they had deposited their tents and baggage in the enclosure of the Alma Bagh, and, leaving an escort to defend it, they were now ready for the struggle of the day, which was to prove the fiercest they had yet encountered.

For some distance from their encampment the road to the town passes through a dense jungle of grass and rank vegetation, six or seven feet high, here and there intersected, chiefly in the background, with clumps of brushwood and trees, while, as it nears the canal which surrounds the more populous part of the city, there are houses enclosed in gardens abutting directly upon the road. As Sir James Outram marched at the head of the first brigade, it became evident that the enemy was bent upon a fierce resistance. No sooner were the British perceived than guns placed in position raked the road with a murderous fire of grape, canister, and round shot, ploughing up the ground and tearing down trees and everything that came in its way, while the sepoy sharpshooters, who filled the jungle, galled the troops, as they approached and passed, with an incessant fire of musketry. After a brief halt for completing the arrangements for an advance, the gallant 5th Fusiliers were ordered to charge the guns. In a few minutes this arduous service was admirably performed, and the enemy's fire was for the moment silenced. But it was only for a moment, for our men had scarcely completed the capture of this outpost when a turn of the road brought them within range of another battery, admirably placed to command the approach and passage of the Char Bagh, a bridge which crosses the canal and forms one of the entrances to the city of Lucknow. The enemy were here in great force. The garden enclosures had been made temporary fortresses, with loopholed walls, from which a constant fire was maintained upon the advancing force. The fire from the heavy guns, which had opened upon them the moment they came within range, was also kept up with terrible energy.

At length, however, the word was given to the British. Then there was a shout, a rush, and a brief struggle, and that battery was theirs. General Outram received a wound in his arm, but during the whole of this fearful day, though faint from loss of blood, nothing could subdue his spirit, and he only dismounted from his horse at the gate of the Residency, when the wonderful passage had been achieved.

During these brilliant affairs the troops had been

harassed by the incessant fire of musketry from the enclosure of the Char Bagh, from the long grass on the left, and from the houses on either side of the street at the town end of the bridge; the rifles almost touching the heads of the artillerymen as they worked the guns, and galling our troops, the more vexatiously because they could not see their foe. That the heavy guns and ammunition waggons, drawn by slow-moving bullocks, might be got across the bridge, it became necessary to clear the garden enclosure, the jungle, and the houses in the town commanding the approach. This was speedily effected, and then the Highlanders were left behind to protect the heavy artillery and baggage-waggons till they were fairly on their way.

Having at length crossed the bridge, the force was now on the direct road to the Residency, distant not much less than two miles; but progress in that direction, for the reasons we have already stated, was impossible. The Generals therefore left the Cawnpore road, and detoured along a narrow lane to the right, which skirts the left bank of the city canal. Their advance was not seriously interrupted until, after a march of some hours, they reached the King's Palace, or Kaizer Bagh.

In the meantime Havelock had become aware that the Highlanders were somewhat in jeopardy at the bridge of the Char Bagh, and he had despatched artillery and cavalry to their aid. The enemy, encouraged by observing their isolated condition when left behind to protect the passage of the bridge soon began to rally from every quarter, occupying the massive buildings on either side of the street, and every corner capable of giving them shelter. Three heavy guns, placed to enfilade the position of the 78th, fired on them with galling accuracy, while from every house-top and every corner a storm of bullets was poured incessantly on this gallant corps. Until every bullock had crossed the bridge they had been ordered not to move, but the fire from the guns threatening their annihilation, and at length becoming insupportable, they determined, as a desperate alternative, to charge the guns and spike them. Led on by their gallant Adjutant, whose horse had already been shot under him, they dashed up the street with a tremendous cheer. They were received with a volley, but, nothing daunted, they charged amidst a furious storm of bullets, and, after a brief struggle, made every one of the guns their own.

The heavy guns and baggage-waggons having passed the bridge, the 78th gathered up their wounded comrades and marched on to join the column then far in advance. But the enemy like bees were on their path; the jungle was in an instant filled with musketeers, while hordes of cavalry hung upon their rear. Through the slow movements of the bullocks their position was yet more critical; when artillery thundered down the street, and they welcomed the succour so opportunely sent them by their General. With a loud cheer the guns were unlimbered, got round and fired, and in an instant the enemy were in retreat. For half a mile they now marched on unmolested, until, having to penetrate the apparently deserted streets, they had again incessantly to encounter enemies of whom they could see nothing save the protruding points of their matchlocks. The fire here thinned their ranks at every step, but they pressed on, till with a hearty cheer they joined their companions under the walls of the Kaiser Bagh.

At this point the fire was tremendous. From heavy artillery, and from the walls swarming with sepoys, the enemy poured down upon the force an iron deluge of grape, canister, and round shot, "under which," wrote Havelock, "nothing could live." They had scarcely silenced this position when they reached a bridge, upon which the foe had again concentrated a murderous fire. At the further end of it they had a battery strongly entrenched, while from other heavy guns an enfilading fire rendered the passage all but inevitable destruction. At a glance the General saw the danger—the word was given—the same rush as of old, the same loud cheer, and the same result,—the bridge batteries were taken and silenced.

It was long past noon when the column reached a place of temporary shelter under the walls of the Furred Buksh. The troops were sorely exhausted. For six weary hours they had struggled in deadly fight with a fierce enemy, and all the while under a scorching sun. Faint and worn out, they endeavoured to snatch a brief respite from this double foe.

Darkness was now coming on, and they were still some distance from the beleaguered garrison, which had all the while listened with bated breath to the cannonade at the Kaizer Bagh. To both the Generals, it was a moment of deep anxiety. Many considerations favoured the plan of occupying the courts of the Mootee Mahul for the night, postponing to the break of day the march to the Residency. Their troops were utterly exhausted with their many hours' fighting, and with the heat; they had many wounded; the transport of the heavy guns and baggage-waggons would greatly retard the progress of the troops in the line of fire through which they had yet to pass. On the other hand, the enemy might congregate during the night in such overwhelming masses, and so completely invest their temporary position, that when the morning came they might find themselves so hemmed in as to be threatened with extermination.* Besides, the garrison was known to be in great extremity. Any hour might seal its ruin. The swarming hordes of Lucknow, said to be fifty thousand strong, ferocious as tigers about to lose their prey, might that night concentrate their fury upon the garrison, and, with the relieving army at its doors, the massacre of Cawn-

* These apprehensions were afterwards ascertained to have been well founded.

pore with all its horrors might be repeated. "I esteemed it to be of such importance," wrote Havelock, "to let the beleaguered garrison know that succour was at hand, that with Sir James Outram's ultimate sanction I directed the main body of the 78th Highlanders and regiment of Ferozepore to advance." After much consideration, for the lives of the men were precious to their Generals, they determined to adopt both alternatives. Leaving the wounded and the baggage and heavy guns with suitable escorts in the Mootee Mahul, and other sheltered places for the night, they placed themselves at the head of the Highlanders and Sikhs, and dashed on for the Residency. No words can picture that march of fire and death! Broad deep trenches had been cut across the road, furnished with every kind of obstruction. Every inch of the way was covered point blank by unseen marksmen; at every turn heavy artillery belched forth its fiery storm of grape and canister. Above, below, everywhere, crowds of human tigers glared from house-top and loop-holed casement upon the intrepid band; while, as they rounded the corner which opened on the squares of the Palace, they had to encounter from many thousand rifles an iron hurricane of destruction and death.

As the brave 78th were passing through an archway, "which literally streamed fire," a bullet struck General Neill on the head, and he fell to rise no more.. The men, enraged, fired a volley against the wall, in the vain hope that some stray bullets might enter the loop-holes, and avenge their brave leader's death. Recalled to their duty by Havelock's word, they marched on, leaving the dying and the dead behind them at every step. It was now dark, but the road was lighted up by the incessant flight of shot and shell, and the furious play of musketry. One obstacle after another was conquered, until the way at last was clear. The gate of the Residency was before them, and with a cheer, which only British soldiers know how to give, the vanguard of Havelock's "Column of Relief" entered, bringing to the beleaguered garrison safety at least, if not deliverance.

And who shall picture the greetings of that night, or describe the joy of those who once more began to hope, and the gratitude they felt to that indomitable deliverer who for nearly a hundred days had struggled through an overwhelming tide of battle, disease, and death, to rescue them from their inhuman foes.

"Our reception," says one, "was enthusiastic,—old men, and women, and wan infants pouring down in one weeping crowd to welcome their deliverers." While another adds, "Many people were nearly mad, and the cheering was deafening."

Since the day that he had been intrusted with the important command he was now about to resign to his gallant friend and fellow-soldier, General

Outram, he had been faithful to his mission. From the time that he had asked his wife to pray that God would enable her husband to "fulfil the expectations of Government," this Christian hero had steadily kept before him the work given him to do, sustained in the execution of his high trust, amidst all his difficulties, by the testimony of a good conscience both towards God and man. And now that his heavenly Master had permitted him to see it accomplished, his gratitude found expression in the words of the Hebrew warrior, "NOT UNTO US, O LORD, NOT UNTO US, BUT UNTO THY NAME DO WE GIVE GLORY."

The next three days brought with them arduous duties. The wounded, with the heavy train, and a number of the troops, were still outside the defences of the Residency. Between them and these objects of their solicitude the Generals knew the enemy would interpose every conceivable obstacle; and as his numbers were counted by tens of thousands, much promptitude and care were needed lest the wounded and their convoys should be overpowered and destroyed.

A party of 250 men was despatched to effect a junction with Colonel Campbell, who had been left with the wounded and the heavy guns in the Mootee Mahul, and to bring in other detached parties, who had been left with suitable escorts on the route of the 25th. Subsequently reinforced the party was able to effect its purpose; but the difficulties it had to contend against will best be indicated by the following graphic narrative from a surgeon attached to the relieving column, who had been left behind on the evening before with one of the parties of wounded:—

"At daybreak the enemy got our range in the building, and kept pouring their shot and shell into us, killing numbers. One poor fellow, an assistant-surgeon in the artillery, was anxious for me to assist him in an operation. I was on my way with him to do it; the shots were whistling all about us. I said, 'Well, Bartrum, I wish I could see my way out of this.' 'Oh,' he said, 'there's no danger whatever.' Next minute he was shot dead beside me. Two minutes before he spoke of the pleasure he expected in rejoining his wife and child in Lucknow. Our situation was now very critical. The enemy were pressing very close, and kept up a storm of shot, shell, and musketry on us. We were cut off from the main body of the army by about a mile, and they could not help us, as they themselves were fighting hard. At last the Colonel came to me, and told me that his arrangements were perfected; he would give me a guard of 150 men, and with them I was to get the wounded into the entrenched camp as best I could. I got the wounded ready in a string, and after a long breath I left the building. For 200 hundred yards the enemy did us no harm, but here we had to cross a deepish nullah—it took me nearly up to my chest; and such a fire we got into here! Some of the wounded were drowned, some killed, but most got across; and on we went to a street where we were promised comparative safety. Our escort preceded us, firing all the way; but they had really no chance, they were shot down right and left. When I got to the entrance of the street I found a number of them lying dead, and most of the others had rushed on for their lives. On looking around I found that the doolie-bearers were being killed from the walls, and the remaining flung down the wounded, and no menace or entreaty could prevail on them to lift them again. I tried to get a few wounded together; but by this time the sepoys had gathered around us on every house-top, and had nothing to do but bring us down at their leisure. All hope seemed gone; but as a last resource I ran with four others into a small one-storeyed house, three rooms on a floor, all doors and windows. Other fugitives now joined us,—soldiers from the escort who had escaped, and two badly wounded officers. The sepoys now commenced yelling fearfully. I calculated their numbers at from 500 to 1000. Their leaders tried to get them to charge down on us, but as often as they came on we gave them a volley, and off went the curs; then they began their yelling again, and reviled us in Hindustanee, telling us that in a few minutes we should be massacred; they were not more than five yards off, but round the corner, and sheltered from our fire. At this time we expected instant death; it seemed incredible that ten effective men could resist 1000, who were firing a fearful hail of shot through the windows. Three of our number inside were struck down wounded, and this diminished our fire. The sepoys all this time were massacring the wounded men in the doolies, (we rescued two more wounded officers and five more wounded men;) perhaps they killed forty by firing volleys at the doolies. The rebels now gave up the attempt to storm us, but crept up to the windows and fired in on us, so we had to lie down on the ground for a time, and let them fire over us; there was no door to the doorway, so we made a barricade of sand bags, by digging the floor with bayonets, and using the dead sepoys' clothes to hold the sand; we also piled up the dead so as to obstruct men rushing on us. My duties, as the only unwounded officer, were to direct and encourage the men —as a surgeon, to dress the wounded—as a man, to use a rifle belonging to a wounded man when he fell. After a while we saw that the enemy were tired of rushing on us; we had killed over twenty of them, and must have wounded many more; this damped them. We now told off one man to fire from each window and three from the door. My post was at a window. I had my revolver, but only five shots left in it. I had no second, and, worst of all, no fresh charges. I must tell you that an Eastern window means a lattice work. At this I kept watch and ward. After a time a sepoy crept up very cautiously, to fire as usual through the window, quite unconscious that at this time a Feringhee had him covered with a revolver. When he got about three yards from me I shot him dead, and another, who was coming up, was shot by one of the men. For nearly an hour now they were very quiet, only firing at a distance. All at once we heard in the street a dull, rumbling noise, which froze me to the very heart. I jumped up, and said, 'Now, men, now or never. Let us rush out and die in the open air, and not be killed like rats in a hole. They are bringing a gun on us.' The men were quite ready, but we now saw that it was not a gun, but something on wheels, with a heavy planking in front too thick for our shot to enter. They brought it to the very window I was firing at. I could touch it, but my shots were useless. To shorten my story, after half-an-hour they set the house in flames, and we were enabled to escape by breaking through into the second room, which opened into a large square, where we found a shed, with large door-ways at intervals; into this we got, carrying our wounded, who, strange to say, were the only ones hurt. Three of them were mortally wounded whilst we were carrying them; we sound men did not get a scratch. It was a complete surprise to the enemy; they expected us by the door, and not by the way we came, so the pleasure of shooting us as we ran from the burning house was denied them, and when they did see us, they, with at least 600 men, only shot three already wounded men. It was now three in the afternoon, and our position seemed hopeless. We thought up to this time that the General would never leave us without succour, but now we thought that the sepoys must have quite hemmed in our army. Imagine our horror when we found that the shed we were in was loopholed everywhere; it had been used the day before as a place to fire on our army from, and the sepoys came creeping up now to the loopholes, firing in suddenly, and off again. We now put a man at every loophole as far as they would go; even wounded were put to watch, and this soon checked the bold, brave sepoy, for whom one British soldier is an object of terrible dread. We soon had a worse alarm. The sepoys got on the roof, bored holes through it, and fired down on us. The first two shots were fired at me, the muzzles of the pieces being perhaps four feet from me, and neither shot hurt me beyond a lot of stuff from the roof being sent with force into my face, and a trifling hurt in my hand. Nothing more wonderful in the way of narrow escapes was ever seen. This could not last; so we bored through the wall of the shed into the courtyard behind, and two of us went cautiously out to reconnoitre. For some time the sepoys did not see us, as it was getting dark. About fifty yards off was a mosque, with no one in it, as I found by creeping on all-fours into it; but before we could get the wounded out we were discovered. We now ran back to the shed. However, we had in the interval secured a chatty of excellent water belonging to the sepoys. And what a prize it was! The wounded were dying with thirst, and we, who had been biting cartridges all day, were just as bad. It gave us one good draught all round, and after it we felt twice the men we did before. Being a long shed, we had a great deal to defend; but luckily the sepoys found out that if they could fire through the roof, so could we, with the advantage of knowing exactly where they were by the noise of their feet; so they kept off the roof. We now organised our defence, told off each man to his alarm-post, and told off the sentries and reliefs. Including wounded, there were nine men fit for sentry, seven men fit to fight, and of these six unhurt, including myself. It was agreed that, if the sepoys forced the shed, we should rush out and die outside. By this time all our wounded were in their possession, and they were put to death, with horrible tortures, actually before our faces; some were burnt alive in the doolies; the shrieks of these men chilled one's blood. The terrors of that awful night were almost maddening; raging thirst, fierce rage against those who, as we thought, had, without an attempt at succour, left us to perish; uncertainty as to where the sepoys would next attack us; add to this, the exhaustion produced by want of food, heat, and anxiety. I now proposed to our men either to fight our way back to the rear-guard, or forward to the entrenched camp; but there were only two who would go, and so I refused to go, as we could not for shame desert eight wounded men; still I tried to persuade all to make the trial; some one might escape; as it was, no one could. Day broke soon after, and we had all fallen into perfect apathy; our nerves, so highly strung for twenty hours, seemed now to have gone quite the other way. Suddenly a few shots were fired outside; then more; then we heard the sharp crack of our own Enfield rifles. Ryan, who was sentry, now shouted 'Oh, boys! them's our own chaps.' Still we were uncertain, till presently we heard a regular rattling volley, such as no sepoy could give. Oh, how our hearts jumped into our mouths then! Up we got; now I said, 'Men, cheer together.' Our people outside heard us, and sent a cheer back. We replied like madmen, and shouted to them to keep off our side. We also fired through all the loopholes at the sepoys, to keep them from firing at our men advancing. In five minutes we were all rescued, and in the midst of our own people; half an hour after we were settled down in the King of Oude's palace —conquerors."

The wounded and the heavy artillery being now safe within the *enceinte* of the Residency, the Generals had quickly to consider their own position and that of the garrison which they had risked so much to relieve. "Our present prospects," wrote General Outram, "have now to be considered. It was the urgent desire of the Government that the garrison should be relieved, and the women and children, amounting to upwards of 470 souls, withdrawn.

"In considering the heavy loss at which we forced our way through the enemy, it was evident that there could be no possible hope of carrying off the sick, wounded, and women and children, (amounting to not less than 1500 souls, including those of both forces.) Want of carriage alone rendered the transport through five miles of disputed suburb an impossibility.

"There remained but two alternatives; one to reinforce the Lucknow garrison with 300 men, and leaving everything behind, to retire immediately with the remains of the infantry upon the Alum Bagh, thereby leaving the garrison in a worse state than we found it, by the addition to the numbers they had previously to feed, the great amount of our wounded, and the 300 soldiers, who would barely have sufficed to afford the additional protection that would have been required, without adding such strength as would have enabled them to make an active defence; to repel attacks by sorties; or to prevent the enemy occupying the whole of their old positions, while it would have been impossible for any smaller force than the remainder of our troops, diminished by those 300 men, to have any hope of making good their way back, and that not without very serious loss. I therefore adopt the second alternative as the only mode of offering reasonable hope of securing the safety of this force, by retaining sufficient strength to enforce supplies of provisions, should they not be open to us voluntarily, and to maintain ourselves, even on reduced rations, until reinforcements advance to our relief."

It will be remembered that up to this date not a soldier either of the Chinese expedition force or of the troops sent out from England had reached Cawnpore. It was therefore not unreasonable, especially now Delhi had fallen, that Outram and Havelock should expect to see strong reinforcements sent to their assistance. They consequently abandoned the intention of removing the wounded, with the women and children, to the Alum Bagh, determining to remain where they were until further help should arrive. It was accordingly arranged that, while Brigadier Inglis retained the command of the original garrison of the Residency, General Havelock and his troops should drive out the enemy, and occupy the palaces extending from the Residency along the river bank, to a point near the Kaiser Bagh. This was effected on the 27th September. Successful sorties were also made on the three following days on the enemy's more advanced positions.

Havelock and his brave force had accomplished a great result. Their arrival had furnished the besieged with a great accession of strength, and thus made them independent of the native troops, upon whose continued fidelity their very existence had for weeks depended. "Our real dangers," writes Lieut. Innes, "consisted in the probable determination of all the natives still with us to abandon us soon—the fearful exhaustion that would consequently have ensued—the necessity of abandoning our outposts—the losses by musketry and mining which would have followed. Opposition to an assault would, with our then diminished numbers, have been next to impossible, and thus most assuredly does the Lucknow garrison owe its lives to the timely arrival of Generals Outram and Havelock and their brave troops."

The relieving column now occupied the series of palaces, in continuation of the Residency, stretching along the banks of the Goomtee. Although much defaced, and everywhere exhibiting the action of war, they still looked grand in their ruin. The gardens, with their ornamental waters, spanned here and there with tasteful bridges; the marble corridors, communicating with the zenanas and gorgeous temples which filled the grounds; the golden domes and fluted minarets towering above the trees, seemed strangely out of keeping with their rude soldier-tenantry. Here were seen a group of rough Highlanders eating their scanty, coarse food out of the finest china, and surrounded with every conceivable article of luxury; and there the dead body of a sepoy or camel polluted the atmosphere, rendering it scarcely bearable. Cashmere shawls and porcelain ornaments lay about unvalued, no one caring to preserve them, whilst of the commonest necessaries there was absolute want. Such is war!

During the interval between the 25th of September, and the final relief of the garrison on November 17, General Havelock continually experienced the extreme difficulty of defending his widely-extended lines with very insufficient means, incessantly harassed, as he was, by an unwearied and subtle foe. Sorties to silence a battery or to gain possession of some outpost of the enemy, were of almost daily occurrence; while, no sooner had he occupied the palaces, than he had to begin a widely-extended system of mining, which required incessant care from him by night and day.

"I am aware of no parallel to our series of mines in modern war," wrote General Outram on the final relief of the garrison; "twenty-one shafts, aggregating 200 feet in depth, and 3291 feet of gallery, have been executed. The enemy advanced twenty mines against the palaces and outposts. Of these they exploded three, which caused us loss of life, and two which did no injury; seven have been blown in; and out of seven others the enemy have been driven, and their galleries taken possession of by our miners;—results of which the Engineer Department may well be proud. The reports and plans forwarded by Sir Henry Havelock, K.C.B., and now submitted to his Excellency, will explain how a line of gardens, courts, and dwelling-houses, without fortified *enceinte*, without flanking defences, and closely connected with the buildings of a city, has been maintained for eight weeks in a certain degree of security; but notwithstanding the close and constant musketry fire from loopholed walls and windows, often within thirty yards, and from every lofty building within rifle range, and notwithstanding a frequent though desultory fire of round shot and grape from guns posted at various distances, from 70 to 500 yards!"

At last, the gunpowder of the garrison began to fail, and something more must be done to counteract the strategy of their cunning enemies. A sort of subterranean cordon, or intercepting mine, was constructed around the more advanced and exposed portion of Havelock's position. Numerous shafts were sunk, and from these, listening galleries were constructed, three feet in height and two feet in breadth, of great length, encircling the whole of that portion of their position open to attack by mining. In these engineers were placed, constantly listening to discover the approach of the enemy's works, that they might break into their mines, or destroy them by small charges of powder, before they could reach Havelock's subterranean boundary. The value of this novel defence, executed under the pressure of an unprecedented exigency, was repeatedly tested, and invariably with the same favourable results. A single instance will shew the arduous nature of this work.

"We broke into their gallery, some twelve feet from our wall, about twelve o'clock at night," says Lieutenant Hutchinson, "and Sergeant Day, our superintending miner, remained below, assisted by others, holding the entrance to their gallery until I arrived.

"On entering the enemy's gallery, I took Corporal Thompson, of the 78th Highlanders, with me, and, observing the apparently great length of the enemy's mine, proceeded cautiously to extinguish the lights, so as to keep ourselves in darkness as we advanced. At this time the enemy were in the mine, at or near their shaft, which, contrary to their usual practice, they evidently wished to hold uninjured. They generally fill them in at once when we take their gallery.

"I proceeded, extinguishing the lights, until I distinctly saw the enemy at the far end, and to advance further would be to advance in a blaze of light. I therefore lay down and waited, as our preparations above, carried on under Lieutenant Tulloch, were not yet ready. Whilst lying there, I saw a sepoy with musket at trail advance down the mine, and when within forty feet of him fired at him. My pistol missed fire, and, before Corporal Thompson could hand me his pistol, the sepoy had retreated. After remaining some time longer, I placed another man with Corporal Thompson, and went up to get an officer down, as I felt it required a very steady man down there to support us. While we were laying the charge, and making various arrangements, which utterly precluded our watching against an enemy's advance at the same time, Lieut. Hay, of the 78th Highlanders, then commanding the picket, kindly volunteered, and took up my old post. Lieut. Tulloch and Sergeant Day quickly got the powder down, and all arrangements ready, when we then withdrew Lieut. Hay behind the partial barricade we had formed; and whilst here, still watching with Corporal Thompson, he got two shots at another man who attemped to come down the mine, and apparently wounded him. The enemy made no more attempts to come down the mine, but went outside their building, and came over our heads, apparently with the intention of breaking through. After some quarter of an hour's walking over head, they, I conclude, could not find the direction of the mine, and retreated into the house.

"Our charge of 50 lbs., which I had laid outside our barricade, and 82 feet up the enemy's gallery, was soon tamped, and the charge fired by Lieutenant Tulloch. The charge being laid with nine feet of sand-bag tamping behind it, and none in front, the main force of the powder acted towards the enemy's shaft, but it took down forty feet backwards towards us, leaving us forty feet to use as a listening gallery. I deduce the enemy's mine to be 200 feet long and upwards, from the reconnoitring of Lieutenant Hay and myself before we commenced laying our charge, and from the position of the houses it came from. The gallery had numerous air-holes, and was thoroughly ventilated."

It was remarkable that Dr Brydon, who was with Havelock under similar desperate circumstances at Jellelabad, was also with him at Lucknow.

A few incidents of these memorable seven weeks were given by the General in a letter, which did not reach Bonn until after the account of his decease. It had been impossible for him to forward any communications, so entirely was his position beleaguered. Only once before in his military experience had he found himself surrounded to such an insuperable extent, and that was at Jellalabad. Even there his isolation was not as extreme as it was at present at Lucknow.

At length there was the hope that he might get tidings of himself and of his son conveyed to their anxious ones on the Rhine, and he wrote accordingly. The letter told in a few words of their dreadful conflict through the city. The severe privations they had been subjected to were intimated rather than narrated. Kindnesses by which they had been cheered were gratefully acknowledged. Expectation of rescue by Sir Colin Campbell was hopefully expressed. There had, alas! been disaster by which his wife and children would be especially distressed. Henry had been wounded amidst the melée, whilst fighting through the city. On hearing what had happened, the husband of his cousin Mary undertook, of his own accord, to go at once and render him what help he could. Too disinterested to calculate what might befall him personally, and too magnanimous to leave his relative to his fate, he sought him out amidst the fire of the foe, and found him seriously damaged in the left arm. He succeeded in bringing him to the Residency, but it was with the loss of his own life. In saving his comrade he had sacrificed himself. One ball struck him, and then another, but on he went with his wounded cousin in his charge, until he had placed him in a place of safety, and then right heroically, with his wife in fullest sympathy with his devotion, he lay down to die.

The letter of the General will be read with the greater interest, as it was the last but one which he wrote to his family:—

"LUCKNOW, *Nov.* 10, 1857.

"You will wonder at not having received a letter by the last two mails. It will be best to begin at the beginning of the story. Sir James Outram brought up my reinforcements on the 18th and 19th September. I threw a noble bridge of boats across the Ganges, and reached the further bank with 2500 men. Sir James announced that I should have the honour of relieving Lucknow, and that he would accompany my force only as Chief Commissioner and as a volunteer. I beat the enemy on the 21st at Mungulwar, and again at Alum Bagh Bhayon on the 23d. . . . . We penetrated through a long suburb, and passed, under the cover of buildings, a fire from the Kaizer Bagh, or King's Palace, under which nothing could have lived. About this time an orderly brought up intelligence that H. was severely wounded. Night was coming on, and Sir James wished to put the troops into a palace and rest them; but I strongly represented the necessity of reinforcing the garrison, lest it should be attacked and surprised in the darkness. So the 78th Highlanders and the Sikh Regiment of Ferozepore were called to the front. Sir James and I, and two of the Staff, put ourselves at their head, and on we charged through streets of loopholed houses, fired at perpetually, and over trenches cut in the road, until we reached in triumph the beleaguered Residency. Then came three cheers from the troops, and the famished garrison found mock-turtle soup and champagne to regale me with as their deliverer. But the rest of my force and guns could not be brought in until the evening of the 26th, and by that time I had lost 535, killed, wounded, and missing. Since that night we have been more closely blockaded than in Jellalabad. We eat a reduced ration of artillery bullock beef, chupatties, and rice; but tea, coffee, sugar, soap, and candles are unknown luxuries. . . . . The noble conduct of Mr Martin Gubbins I must next record. My head-quarters were established in the house of the late Mr Ommaney, who was killed during the siege. Gubbins sent to invite me and all my staff to come and live in his better house. To this I would not consent, but commended to his care my two wounded officers, Col. Tytler and H., and he has cared for them as if they were his children. I dine with him once a-week, and he keeps me supplied with excellent sherry, without which it would have gone ill with me, for I find it not so easy to starve at sixty-three as at forty-seven. The enemy fire at us perpetually with guns, mortars, and musketry, but our casualties are not very numerous . . . . . I should have told you that Bensley Thornhill volunteered to go out and bring H. in. Alas! he received one bad wound over the eye, which injured the skull, whilst another ball broke in pieces his right arm. It was amputated. He lingered many days, and then died in the hospital, leaving Mary a young widow. Their only infant had died some time before. We are now daily expecting Sir Colin Campbell. . . . . I visit the whole of my posts in the palaces and gardens with my Staff, on foot, daily; but my doctor has advised me to take something strengthening until we can get upon good diet again."

The following announcement of the death of the gallant Thornhill contains the particulars of his decease:—

"Died at Lucknow on the 12th of October 1857, from wounds received on the 26th of September, when nobly heading a party to bring in some wounded men that had been left behind when Generals Outram and Havelock forced their way into the Residency on the previous evening, J. Bensley Thornhill, Esq., of the Bengal Civil Service, aged twenty-five years and six months. He had got in all the wounded except twelve men, and was taking the eldest son of General Sir Henry Havelock into a place of safety when wounded, and as he entered a gateway a sepoy from the opposite house sent a ball through his right arm; he tied his handkerchief round his shattered arm, and went on with his noble and humane duty, and when returning the same sepoy fired at him again, the ball wounding him over the temple, and leaving him insensible. He was taken to the hospital, and his right arm was amputated that night. He lingered sixteen days, and died of exhaustion from loss of blood, and want of food and nourishment that the place was destitute of. He was previously twice wounded in the heroic defence of the Lucknow garrison, and was honourably named in General Inglis's despatch of the 25th of September. He will be sincerely lamented by all who were acquainted with his upright and Christian character. He has left a young widow of eighteen, (a niece of the brave General Sir Henry Havelock,) who has to mourn the loss of both her husband and infant child, after all the privations and suffering she endured with the heroic garrison at Lucknow. Her husband got his death-wound in doing a brave, humane, and Christian act; and had he lived, the highest honour—that of the Victoria Cross—would have been his. This is some consolation to her, and to his widowed mother."

The sagacity of Havelock's medical man had observed for some time that the General's strength was on the wane. No actual surrendering had he evinced, either to any sense of lassitude or to any demand for repose. A dominant will peremptorily insisted on the suppression of any complaint, and on the unfaltering employment of every power both of body and mind. More necessary than ever were his vigilance and his energy both day and night. They must, therefore, be maintained. It was kind of the doctor to put him on his guard; still he had no option—he must go on.

But he must at his time of life be cautious. The privations of the last few weeks had considerably weakened him, and the extraordinary fatigue which he had undergone rendered it rather urgently incumbent that he should take care. There were symptoms, he was assured, which it would be most unwise to overlook.

He had no desire to overlook them. He would take what care he could. At the same time, even if heart and flesh should fail, he must do his duty to his country, and that demanded from him just now he vigilant protection of the Residency from its ruthless and raging foes.

CHAPTER XVII.

THE RESCUE ACCOMPLISHED.

TIME had been wearing on. October had passed, and November was now dragging its days and weeks anxiously along; the hopes of the garrison meanwhile existing as they best could upon the scanty intelligence brought in by spies, or communicated to them through a semaphore that had been extemporised upon the roof of the Alum Bagh. About the 12th of November they were made acquainted with the advance of Sir Colin Campbell from Cawnpore, and of his junction with Brigadier Grant's column then on its way to Lucknow; and on the evening of the same day they heard of his arrival at the Alum Bagh. On the 15th the march of the General to the Residency with a force of 5000 men was telegraphed, and from that moment every one was on the watch to mark his progress. Regardless of the danger, courageous spirits mounted to the tower of the Residency, while not a few joined the look-out on the top of the Post-office. Here they were able to mark his course, while the smoke and fire indicated plainly his steady advance to their relief.

Instead of crossing the canal at the bridge of the Char Bagh, as Havelock had done, on leaving the Alum Bagh Sir Colin at once diverged to the right, crossing the country to the Dilkoosha, a small palace surrounded by gardens, about three miles from the Residency. The different routes may easily be traced on the map, at page 270. The sun was in its strength, and the march lay through meadow land and young sugar canes, but the troops, inspired with the iron energy of their leader, made light of these obstacles. After a running fight of two hours they drove the enemy down the park to the Martiniere, leaving that building, as well as the Dilkoosha, in the hands of Sir Colin Campbell. From this point his course to the Residency was successively disputed by the enemy, entrenched in great force in a series of strongly-fortified buildings.

Early next morning Sir Colin began his march on the Sikunder Bagh, a strong square building, surrounded by a wall of solid masonry—as usual, loopholed all round. It was evident that the enemy had formed here in great numbers, and that the possession of the place would be hotly contested. A village on the opposite side of the road was also held by them. It was necessary at once to reduce the building, and to drive the enemy from the village. The General saw that to effect this, artillery was wanted in a position that could not be reached without passing between a raking crossfire from the village and the Sikunder Bagh itself. But there was no alternative. The necessary orders were therefore given, and in a moment two batteries, one of the Bengal, and another of the Royal Artillery, were galloping their guns through a merciless stream of fire. This done, a dazzling line of bayonets, belonging to the 53d and to the Highlanders, closed round the loop-holed village, and cleared it at a run. Ahead of these two regiments the mutineers occupied ground on the left of our advance in deep masses; but neither the strength of their ranks nor their numbers were of any avail against our brave soldiers. They swept across the ground without firing until they just faced the enemy; then came the sharp gleam of fire, and the quick rattle, as of a single shot, and the bayonet in its terrible strength did all the rest. The mutineers were dispersed and driven across the plain, the 53d chasing them in skirmishing order, while the 93d, seizing the abandoned barracks, turned them into a military post.

"The sight from the Residency," says an eyewitness, "was very fine. We could observe the enemy retiring, and our guns advancing, through openings in the trees. Occasionally a staff officer was seen dashing across, and once a group of mounted officers, supposed to be Sir Colin and his staff, appeared and disappeared again. The firing of heavy guns, and the smoke rising in the clear air, with occasional glimpses of the troops, added greatly to the effect of a naturally beautiful landscape."

Meanwhile the artillery had been battering the walls of the Sikunder Bagh with little effect. At last a breach was made—a hole of two feet square, not more,—and then began a charge which for heroic daring has never been surpassed, and rarely equalled. The Sikhs and Highlanders rushed to the wall, and through that hole—for breach it could not be called—they dragged themselves in upon the foe. The entrance once effected, woe to the mutineers! From the prison they had chosen there was no escape, except through barred windows high up in the building, and through the barricaded gate which was within a few yards of the cannon's mouth. What passed within that house of horrors none who survive care to tell. None of them, indeed, can tell,—so intensely was every man absorbed with his own onset and onslaught with the foe. Everything seemed concentrated on himself and his exploits.

Hour after hour passed in that awful struggle. As we read of the storming of the Sikunder Bagh, it may seem as if it had been the work of a little while. It was the work of the best part of the whole day. Anxious men stood round this crater outside, wondering how the battle sped and when it would be won.

The volcano within the thick walls still raged

like a fiery furnace, and life was its costly fuel. Gradually the sphere of action widened as different parts of the building were carried and allowed the entrance of fresh men; but not more than four hundred soldiers of our army were at any moment inside; and, once in, there was no egress. The mutineers, whose numbers were at first overwhelming, struggled hard for life. At last they were put down; the work of death was done; the Sikunder Bagh no more intercepted the march of mercy; and as our countrymen looked on the piles of the disfigured dead, they were constrained to say, "Here is retribution for Cawnpore."

Sir Colin's march was next opposed by the Shah Nujjeef, a mosque, surrounded by a garden, protected by a strong wall. "The wall of the enclosure of the mosque," says Sir Colin, "was loopholed with great care. The entrance to it had been covered by a regular work in masonry, and the top of the building was crowned with a parapet. From this, and from the defences in the garden, an unceasing fire of musketry was kept up from the commencement of the attack.

"This position was defended with great resolution against a heavy cannonade of three hours. It was then stormed in the boldest manner by the 93d Highlanders, under Brigadier Hope, supported by a battalion of detachments, under Major Barnston, who was, I regret to say, severely wounded; Captain Peel leading up his heavy guns with extraordinary gallantry within a few yards of the building, to batter the massive stone walls. The withering fire of the Highlanders effectually covered the Naval Brigade from great loss; but it was an action almost unexampled in war. Captain Peel behaved very much as if he had been laying the *Shannon* alongside an enemy's frigate.

"This brought the day's operations to a close."

No pen can describe the engrossing interest with which Sir Colin's progress had been watched by the garrison. They could see every step he took, and they marked how every impediment raised by the enemy was overcome, until he reached the Sikunder Bagh and the mosque, while every gun he fired wakened an echo in many an anxious heart among those whom he was hastening to relieve.

Meanwhile, Generals Outram and Havelock had been making every preparation to co-operate when he should approach near enough for them to act with safety to their own position.

The following extracts from Havelock's last despatch, narrating these operations, will now be read with melancholy interest:—

"The progress of the relieving force under his Excellency the Commander-in-Chief was anxiously watched, and it was determined that as soon as he should reach the Sikunder Bagh, about a mile and a-half from the Residency, the outer wall of the advance garden of the palace, in which the enemy had before made several breaches, should be blown in by the mines previously prepared; that two powerful batteries erected in the enclosure should then open on the insurgents' defences in front; and after the desired effect had been produced, that the troops should storm two buildings known by the names of the Hern-khana, or Deer-house, and the Steam Engine-house. Under these, also, three mines had been driven.

"It was ascertained, about eleven A.M., that Sir Colin Campbell was operating against the Sikunder Bagh. The explosion of the mines in the garden was therefore ordered. Their action was, however, comparatively feeble, so the batteries had the double task of completing the demolition of the wall and prostrating and breaching the works and the buildings beyond it. Brigadier Eyre commanded in the left battery; Captain Olpherts in the right; Captain Maude shelled from six mortars in a more retired quadrangle of the palace. The troops were formed in a square of the Chuttur Munzill, and brought up in succession through the approaches, which in every direction intersected the advance garden. At a quarter-past three two of the mines at the Hern-khana exploded with good effect. At half-past three the advance sounded. It is impossible to describe the enthusiasm with which this signal was received by the troops. Pent up in inaction for upwards of six weeks, and subjected to constant attacks, they felt that the hour of retribution and glorious exertion had returned.

"Their cheers echoed through the courts of the palace, responsive to the bugle sound, and on they rushed to assured victory. The enemy could nowhere withstand them. In a few minutes the whole of the buildings were in our possession, and have since been armed with cannon, and steadily held against all attack."

"On the next day," (we now quote from Sir Colin's despatch,) "communications were opened to the left rear of the barracks to the canal, after overcoming considerable difficulty. Captain Peel kept up a steady cannonade on the building called the mess-house. This building, of considerable size, was defended by a ditch about twelve feet broad, and scarped with masonry, and beyond that a loopholed mud wall. I determined to use the guns as much as possible in taking it.

"About three P.M., when it was considered that men might be sent to storm it without much risk, it was taken by a company of the 90th Foot, under Captain Wolseley, and a picquet of her Majesty's 53d, under Captain Hopkins, supported by Major Barnston's battalion of detachments, under Captain Guise, her Majesty's 90th Foot, and some of the Punjaub Infantry, under Lieutenant Powlett. The mess-house was carried immediately with a rush.

"The troops then pressed forward with great vigour, and lined the wall separating the mess-house from the Motee Mahal, which consists of a wide enclosure and many buildings. The enemy here made a last stand, which was overcome after an hour, openings having been broken in the wall, through which the troops poured, with a body of sappers, and accomplished our communications with the Residency.

"I had the inexpressible satisfaction, shortly afterwards, of greeting Sir James Outram and Sir Henry Havelock, who came out to meet me before the action was at an end.

"The relief of the besieged garrison had been accomplished."

What a greeting was that! The iron chief, Sir Colin, with the dust of battle still upon him, the "good Sir James," and the dying Havelock. Meeting, too, while the walls of the palace where they stood were still reverberating with the din of battle;—fit atmosphere for that reunion! True knights these three brave hearts! Each had perilled his life to rescue the helpless, and one was soon to lay his down, worn out in their defence.

"Sir Colin Campbell," (says the author of "The Siege of Lucknow,") "received the hearty thanks and congratulations of Sir James with evident satisfaction; and General Havelock, not less delighted and proud, harangued the troops who had so gallantly carried out all the Commander-in-Chief's brilliant manœuvres, in that concise, and yet soul-stirring language for which he was so well known by his soldiers. While yet speaking, his attention was drawn to the place where his eldest son had just fallen, wounded by a musket ball from the enemy. Though his father's heart must have been then bleeding with anguish, and beating with curiosity to know the nature of the wound, the General, with wonderful self-command, continued his discourse without interruption, and then, only amidst the cheers of the men who were unacquainted with the sad event which had just happened, left to visit his wounded son. Fortunately it was only a slight wound, and he soon recovered from the effects of it."

It now became necessary to consider in what way the removal from the Residency could be accomplished. To have stayed there would have been to insure the recurrence of the hardships and disasters of the last seven weeks. They must depart without delay. It was determined by Sir Colin Campbell to effect his object by a *ruse.* He made his dispositions accordingly, continuing his fire, as if he intended to dislodge the enemy from their position around the Residency. Through several days in succession this was done. In the meantime lines of picquets were being arranged, through which the women and children with the wounded were to be conducted to the Alum Bagh. Of this the rebels had no information, so that they kept on their murderous fire, as they deemed it, upon the garrison far into the night. Before midnight on the 19th November the departure had commenced. Leaving behind them many a sad memento of the losses they had suffered and of the calamities they had endured, the rescued ones went forth, hardly knowing whither they went. Probabilities were all against the hope that they might elude the observation of their fiendish and bloodthirsty foes. But greater was He who was for them than all those who were against them. The cavalcade moved silently and slowly onwards, unnoticed and unchallenged by any portentous token or any unfriendly voice. Believing that the picquets were faithfully occupying their appointed places, and that the pathways along the many narrow lanes had been well ascertained, hope animated the fugitives, whilst the continuous fire upon their abandoned prison-house convinced them the assailants had no idea of their escape. The Generals were as anxious and as vigilant as though they had had their own wives and children beneath their care, evincing the most instinctive solicitude to secure as far as possible the convenience of each wounded soldier, and the comfort of every weakly child. A fine subject for a congenial artist that strange and extemporaneous grouping of young men and maidens, of old men and children, threading their dubious way from impending danger to a place of safety amidst the darkness of a long November night.

It had been deemed necessary to take from the Residency the treasure which had been accumulated there, and the jewels formerly belonging to the King of Oude; this was following in the train of the cavalcade. Hour after hour passed without the occurrence of a mishap, and as morning drew on the impression deepened and encouraged every heart that they were really safe. Daylight at length revealed to them their position, and they saw the picquets, between whose friendly and effective shelter they had been passing all the night, closing in around them in strictest order. To the delight of the gallant deliverers, not a soul who had left Lucknow was missing. One of the most sagacious devices with which modern warfare is acquainted was completely successful. The hope that had been so long deferred was realised; thus far the fugitives from the house of bondage were free. A subsequent march under the same truly patriarchal guardianship brought the rescued ones to the Alum Bagh. Having obtained what refreshment was available for their manifold need, the wounded and the sick, with the children and women, were escorted towards Cawnpore, on their way to Allahabad; God still wonderfully preserving them and honouring as with His special favour the self-denying and indomitable bravery which twice over had interposed for their relief. Happy was Havelock beyond expression as he bade the objects of his anxiety and the companions of his privations farewell. They were on their way, he trusted, to scenes at once peaceful and secure; he would remain and fulfil his duty, that in time to come the scenes about Lucknow might be peaceful and secure too. The day would dawn on India when they should beat their swords into ploughshares and their spears into pruning-hooks, when nation would not lift up sword against nation, neither should they learn war any more,—when, to adopt his own words, "the evils and horrors of belligerency" would be unknown.

CHAPTER XVIII.

HAVELOCK'S PEACEFUL DEATH.

BEFORE the rescue had been quite accomplished, Havelock had become seriously unwell. The first symptoms which excited immediate apprehension were those of indigestion. These, however, were presently suppressed, and he was pronounced better. There seemed cause for hope; especially as he was not only now relieved from his heavy responsibility, but was provided with the wholesome sustenance of which he had for weeks been deprived. His medical attendant was most assiduous; and, from the Commander-in-Chief down to the servants in the Residency, all were ready to render to the General any help within their power.

The 20th of November closed upon him with some promise of continuous amendment; but before midnight, according to a correspondent of *The Englishman*, unmistakable signs of dysentery made their appearance, and promptest attention was necessary, with the best measures which sagacity and science could supply. They were apparently successful; and by the forenoon of the 21st there were again indications of improvement.

With characteristic mindfulness of home, one of the first things which he had done on the relief of the Residency was to write to his family. Other letters had indicated apprehension of what might happen. This letter expresses nothing which gave occasion for alarm.

Prospects were brightening, and he hoped that they should ere long bear away the surviving women and children to a place of safety, and that some of their own most pressing wants would in a measure be supplied. For weeks had they been unable to change any of their clothing. Just as they came into the Residency so had they continued night and day for forty days; harassed incessantly by the enemy, and beset with disease and death, without even the ordinary conveniences whereby they could be bodily refreshed. It would be better now.

Information, too, had reached him of the estimate in which his country held him for his bravery, and of the first of the series of honours which had been conferred on him by the Queen. This was cheering. He was grateful, but as modest and unostentatious as ever. The children were remembered in a kindly message, and their brother, they were assured, though again wounded, was doing well:—

"*Nov.* 19.—Sir Colin has come up with some

5000 men, and much altered the state of affairs. The papers of the 26th September came with him, announcing my elevation to the Commandership of the Bath for my first three battles. I have fought nine more since. . . . . Dear H. has been a second time wounded in the same left arm. This second hit was a musket-ball in the shoulder. He is in good spirits, and is doing well. . . . . Love to the children. . . . . I do not after all see my elevation in the *Gazette*, but Sir Colin addresses me as Sir Henry Havelock. . . . . Our baggage is at Alumbagh, four miles off; and we all came into this place with a single suit, which hardly any have put off for forty days."

This was the last letter which Havelock ever wrote. No more would he indite the graver or the pleasanter things for perusal and pleasurable conversation at Bonn. Henceforward the wedding-day and the birthdays would pass uncommemorated by the grateful references of the conjugal and parental pen. The admonitions and encouragements which had been so habitually interspersed with the periodical correspondence of the last seven years had come to a perpetual end. Happily, however, though his communications with his beloved ones had terminated, they would hear that his confidence in God had triumphantly availed as he passed through the valley of the shadow of death.

It was now generally known that Havelock was getting worse. He was not seen about among his companions-in-arms. They missed him in the places of military resort. There was sorrow lest, after all his self-sacrificing exertions to rescue others, he should himself succumb.

To further the incipient improvement of the 20th, it had been arranged to move him to the Dilkoosha; the change of air being deemed of importance at the crisis which he had just reached.

Well aware was he of the danger that was impending. Yet, whilst he felt his jeopardy to be extreme, he was thoroughly calm. The peace of God which passeth all understanding was keeping his heart and mind through Jesus Christ. If he were about to pass through the valley of the shadow of death, he would fear no evil. Why should he? There were the rod and the staff to comfort him. There was "the Resurrection and the Life" awaiting to be the strength of his heart, and his portion for ever. How often had he cheered his brethren by the assurances of life and immortality when they were in thickest danger! How many times had he talked of Providence, of everlasting purposes, of the keys of Hades and of Death, of the destruction of the last enemy, of departure to be with Christ! With his Bible in his hand had he made good the statement that the believer in the Son of God cannot be too confident of all-sufficient help whenever he may come to die.

And now, relying on the exceeding great and precious promises, he was strong in faith. The sting of death, so far as he was personally concerned, had been destroyed. Death itself had been abolished. Life and immortality had been brought to light. His gracious Lord had once been within the power of the last enemy. And what had he done with Him? Had he retained Him within his grasp? Could he boast of perpetual dominion over Him? Was Jesus still amidst the degradation of the Arimathean tomb?

Oh, how the Christian veteran on his couch understood the triumphant answer to such inquiries! and how, as he remembered his Master's words, "I was dead, but I am alive again; and, behold, I am alive for evermore," he sang with melody in his heart, "Because He lives, I shall live also!"

True, the earthly house of his tabernacle must be dissolved. The grave would receive THAT into its dark and desolate domain: but it would not receive HIM. He should not die. He should not see corruption. There would be no cessation of his being; no intermission of his existence; no interruption of his life. His consciousness would be continued, as would also his character, and his fellowship and union with Christ. Before his son, who was so considerately attending on him, could say that his father was no more, he would be singing, amidst the exulting impulses of his incipient immortality, "Thanks be unto God, who hath given me the victory, through our Lord Jesus Christ."

So he mused and meditated, mingling faith with

what had been so familiar to him in the Scripture readings and exhortations of upwards of forty years. He had not believed in vain. Strength from heaven was made perfect in his weakness. The Master whom he had served and trusted was at his right hand.

The change from the Residency had refreshed the invalid. Further improvement was observed, and gladly reported. It might be that, though terribly reduced, he would survive. Only momentary was the probability. Early on the 22d the disease assumed a malignant form ; and though it inflicted no sevère bodily suffering, yet it was evidently taking away his life.

The confidence of the dying man became more and more profound. To have departed in the midst of his family would have been an alleviation. Thoughts, fond and fatherly, followed one another towards his beloved ones far away on the Rhine. But God had willed that he should not go hence with their prayerful and sustaining utterances falling gently on his ear. He therefore devoutly acquiesced; and, remembering gracious promises about God's inalienable loving-kindness to the fatherless and the widow, he commended them to the Divine care, and then collected himself to enjoy the abundant entrance into the everlasting kingdom of our Lord and Saviour Jesus Christ.

The 23d passed in the calmest submission to the Lord's will. Every faculty was active, and every sensibility of his nature in fullest power. No mere indifference was upon him. It was not because he did not choose to realise his position that he contrived to be at peace. He knew that he was about to make the great transition from the life that now is to that which is to come. He remembered his unworthiness of all God's favours. He was actually conscious, as he was lying there in his prostration, of his personal desert of banishment from God. But then he was in Christ; and, being there, it was impossible he should perish. He must needs have everlasting life.

His illustrious companion, Sir James Outram, having called, he thought it right to say to him what was then upon his mind. "For more than forty years," was his remark to Sir James,—"for more than forty years I have so ruled my life that when death came I might face it without fear."

Often had they faced it together, even during that recent memorable advance for the relief of Lucknow. There, however, God had averted it; but here, at the Dilkoosha, it was present in all its power, and must be met. "So be it," was the unperturbed response of Outram's comrade; "I am not in the least afraid. To die is gain."

"I die happy and contented," he kept on saying, knowing whom he had believed, and persuaded that he was able to keep what he had committed to him until that day.

On the 24th his end was obviously near at hand.

His eldest son was still his loving and faithful nurse; —himself, it should be remembered, a wounded man, and specially needing kindly care. Waiting on his father with unflagging and womanly assiduity, he was summoned to hearken to some parting words.

"Come," said the disciple thus faithful unto death; "come, my son, and see how a Christian can die."—And Havelock died.

"HAVING SERVED HIS OWN GENERATION, BY THE WILL OF GOD, HE FELL ON SLEEP."

On the 25th a grave was prepared for his remains in the Alum Bagh, and Sir Colin Campbell, with his sorrowing comrades who had followed him through so many vicissitudes, buried him out of sight, in sure and certain hope of the resurrection unto eternal life.

"There gleams a coronet of light around our Hero's brow,
But of far purer radiance than England could bestow.
He takes his place among his peers. His peers! And who are they?
Princes of yon celestial spheres, whom angel hosts obey.
The heralds have made search, and found his lineage of the best,
He stands amidst the sons of God, a son of God confess'd!
He wears a glittering, starry cross, call'd by a Monarch's name;
That Monarch whose 'Well done' confers a more than mortal fame.
Victorious at Futtehpore,—victorious at Lucknow,
The gallant chief of gallant men is *more* than conqueror now!

For his whole life was one stern fight against so fierce a foe,
That only superhuman might avails to lay him low.
And he possess'd a talisman, through which he won the day;
A blood-red signature which kept the hosts of hell at bay.
The banner under which he served can never know defeat,
And so he lays his laurels down at his great Captain's feet.
There rest thee, Christian Warrior,—rest from the twofold strife—
The battle-fields of India, and the battle-field of life!
Rest in the presence of thy Lord, where trouble may not come,
Nor thy repose be broken through by sound of hostile drum;
There, where no flaming sun beats down on the unshelter'd head;
Where no pale moon keeps mournful watch over the silent dead!
And when, in years to come, men's thoughts to this dark time are turn'd,
And the bright stars are reckon'd up which in its midnight burn'd,
Then shall the name of Havelock, the saintly, sage, and bold,
Shine forth engraven on the rock in characters of gold!"

CHAPTER XIX.

CONCLUSION.

HAVELOCK'S letters and despatches enable us to form an accurate estimate of the man. It was quite his purpose to be understood. From the ambiguous and the diplomatic he was remarkably free. His correspondence was characteristic, and, like his countenance and general bearing, it went far to shew exactly what he was. His personal presence was indicative, and the productions of his pen were significant. The fire of his eye, and the promptitude of his utterance, and the elasticity of his step induced opinions which were immediately confirmed by the quickness of his perception, the readiness of his rejoinder, and the expressiveness of his style. There was no secretiveness about him, and he was pre-eminently sincere. Appearances and realities agreed.

His example thus becomes safely available for imitation through the incidents and the letters of this brief biographic sketch. To peruse them is to understand his character, and to examine them is to admire his excellences—to regard him, indeed, as in some points of paramount interest a proximately model man.

His diligence in his professional duties was remarkable. Having become a soldier with the full consent of his judgment, he was from first to last punctually and promptly at his post. Through his long and chequered military career he had never to meet an accusation or to answer a complaint. Though watched by unfriendly eyes for years together, with a view to his dishonour before his comrades, he survived the ordeal triumphantly, and, as Sir Archibald Campbell put it, "Havelock was always ready." Whatever he did he did with his might—a pattern, not to military men only, but to all other men as well. The dilatory and the double-minded have only to look carefully at the portrait, and to ruminate upon some passages of the life, to be effectively reproved. Where would the well-earned baronetcy have been, had the Baronet of Lucknow lazily postponed the duties of to-day until to-morrow? Where would the successes of Jellalabad and Futtehpore have been, had not obligations been discharged as they successively arose? "No arrears" was a great maxim of Havelock's. Is it incumbent? Then it must be done forthwith.

He aimed, too, to ascertain what from time to time was incumbent. He was an observer of circumstances, and a thinker upon them in their relation to his principles of action. Reading was kept up. Experience was treasured. Mental discipline was maintained. For emergencies he was prepared —even for such emergencies as he had more than once suddenly to meet! Though always prompt he was never reckless. Diligence and discrimination were combined.

Havelock had obviously great enjoyment of life, evincing not, perhaps, the lighter or the more superficial moods of cheerfulness so much as those which are quieter and more profound. It delighted him to examine works of art, and he was reckoned to no small extent a connoisseur. On the picturesque and the sublime in nature he was accustomed to gaze with admiration, and for the expression of his emotions he availed himself of the finer poetry that he was familiar with from the inspired as well as from uninspired books. Intelligent society was ever agreeable to him, and, though not amongst the foremost talkers of his acquaintance, he entered with great zest into current conversation, appreciating somewhat keenly the sentiment of the wise man, that "as iron sharpeneth iron, so a man sharpeneth the countenance of his friend." No quotation can the ascetic or the recluse make from any of the sayings or the doings of Havelock in defence of his avoidance of society. From the foregoing pages he may learn how a man may use the world without abusing it. If he read and understand and sympathise, he will go and mingle with his neighbours that he may instruct and be instructed, that he may entertain and be entertained.

Nothing can be plainer than that Havelock was a dear lover of his wife and children. Let him once find himself with them, and, as he used to say, he was "as happy as a duck in thunder." The ringing laugh of his boys often led him with heartiest humour to join in their hilarity, and when his girls could get him to take part in their amusements their enjoyment was complete. He won their entire confidence by his sympathy, and was often lightened of his cares by the unceremonious and very unsophisticated manifestations of their love.

Even during the last long separation of seven years this feeling of warm attachment was kept up by the confessedly trying process of written correspondence. It survived a trial as severe as that. The arrival of the letters from Bonn was looked for with anxiety and hailed with delight. The answering of the letters was the greatest pleasure of the month. Clerks were sent to the right about, and "business was pitched out of the windows" for the time being. The picture that had just come out must be duly criticised. Little H.'s minute mistakes in orthography must be corrected. A recent visit to "the monumental slab, sacred to your dear mother's memory," must be reported. Anything and everything that had made up the lifetime of the last month on the Ganges or the Jumna was stereotyped and sent off that it might be lived over again on the Rhine. The assurances which he received he reciprocated. The pledges of unabated affection which never failed to reach him from Europe he never forgot to return from India. Conjugal and parental responsibilities were maintained by him untarnished and intact. It was not within the power of any comrade, who might resent his exhortations about the world-wide obligation of the domestic sanctities, to silence him with the taunt, "Physician, heal thyself."

When tempted, and most plausibly tempted, to forget that obligation, the admirers of Havelock may peradventure call his example up to mind, and behave as he behaved towards their wives and children. The vows which bound him bind them. The grace of God, which was sufficient to keep him unspotted from the world, is sufficient to keep them. No reason is there whatsoever why every soldier and every civilian in India and elsewhere should not be the pure-minded and virtuous man.

Havelock had no dispute with the man who insisted that every act of our daily life should be a religious act. It was one of his own most cherished principles that a man ought to be as virtuous and godly amidst the occupations of the world as in the services of the Church.

But virtue needed to be reinvigorated and godliness to be renewed by means which it had pleased his Heavenly Father to provide. He therefore used those means most diligently, and, instead of losing himself in vague generalities, he sought first the kingdom of God and His righteousness. From the outset he had cogent reasons for re-examining the necessity and the propriety of his habit. Persecution for righteousness' sake early threatened him. He would find it far pleasanter on many accounts to keep aloof from the fanatics than to associate with them. To be "righteous over much" was not the way for a military man to win either promotion or applause. Discipleship in secret was in his circumstances the safer thing.

He was unmoved by all such expostulations: the higher consideration prevailing, that it was his business, at all hazards, to obey God. The consequence was, that society has seldom seen a more unequivocal case of religious profession. It was begun on board the *General Kyd*, and it was maintained through numerous and trying vicissitudes to the hour of his death.

He was not all day long at his Bible, but he invariably pondered some portion of it every day. He was not continually in the outward act of prayer, but he took care, somehow or other, to be alone both morning and evening, that he might worship and bow down. He was not constantly at church or chapel, but he was there on the Lord's-day, and not unfrequently on other days besides. If for these engagements he could not find time, he made time. Even when so pressed as he was at Jellalabad, he got his comrades who were like-minded with himself together constantly that they might join in worshipping and in commending themselves to God; and when on his heaviest marches it was determined to start at some earlier hour than that which he had fixed for his devotions, he arose quite in time to hold undisturbed his usual fellowship with God. He lived and he died, declaring that where there is a will there is a way.

No doubt was there of the preference which he cherished for one of the various bodies of which the Church of Christ is now composed. His correspondence and his conversations made his denominational peculiarities plain. He was a Nonconformist, not a Churchman; a Baptist, not a Pedobaptist; a Calvinist, not an Arminian. But he was, at the same time, and always, not a bigot, but a brother. Every Christian body might rely on his cooperation. Every Christian family might be sure of his sympathy. Every Christian Church might reckon on his presence in the celebration of the Supper of the Lord. Enough for him that a man or a community loved the Lord Jesus in sincerity. If they would allow him, he was ready to shew himself their coadjutor and their friend.

A fine specimen was Havelock of a Christian professor. He deemed it imperative on him to take a different position from the generality of his neighbours. Having been made to differ—as he believed—he thought it right to avow the difference. Without any arrogance, he reckoned himself one of a peculiar people, whose business it was to be zealous of good works. The enemies of the cross of Christ were banded together in manifold expression of their animosity: he felt that the friends of that cross should confederate together in token of their attachment. And what good man will not feel the same, especially when he reads the oft-repeated injunctions of Holy Scripture to present his body a living sacrifice to God? No option is left to "a disciple indeed." He is required to become a marked man. The injunction is that he take his place on the Lord's side. Christ is to be confessed before man.

Should any reader of this book feel that this responsiblity rests on himself, and yet should he be perplexed by the difficulties which a profession apparently involves, let him read again, and learn from Havelock that sanctimoniousness is no element of saintship—that fanaticism and Christian fellowship are essentially different things—that a man's loyalty to his earthly sovereign is most congenially compatible with loyalty to the Lord his God, who will never fail to fulfil His promise—"Him that honoureth Me I will honour."

Havelock had strong convictions of the good man's duty concerning the salvation of those with whom he has influence. Having men under his authority, he felt himself bound to instruct them on the subject of religion: supplementing rather than interfering with the labours of other servants of the Lord.

Most sincerely did he esteem all faithful ministers of Christ. Upon the services which they conducted was he a constant attendant, whenever he had the opportunity. For a stated and settled administration, both of the word and ordinances of the gospel, he evinced the highest possible respect. In no degree would he heedlessly infringe upon what he always held to be an institution of the Head of the Church. At the same time, when those around him were perishing for lack of knowledge, and there were none ready to interfere to prevent the consummation of the calamity, he felt constrained to interfere himself. The fact that, in the apostolic times, men who were not specially ordained went everywhere preaching the Word, came up to his recollection; and, as the result, he felt that, under the circumstances, he must preach. He could expound to the inquiring the meaning of Christ's gracious invitations, and he could enforce upon the thoughtless the lessons of Christ's solemn admonition. He began the effort and continued it to the last; often, if not in every case, most diligently preparing his discourses, in order by the manifestation of the truth to commend himself to every man's conscience in the sight of God.

What urgent need of similar efforts is accumulating on every side! The ministers of the gospel of every name have their incumbent duty pressing more weightily than ever, and Christian laymen are summoned to render them their personal cooperation and undivided aid. There is hardly a village or a parish in the kingdom where the necessity does not exist. There is not a ship that goes to sea in which this evangelic effort may not properly be made. The sphere can scarcely be conceived of where an opportunity does not offer every day for saying to some unenlightened neighbour, "Know you the Lord." Happy the day for England and for the world at large when, without waiting for any ordination or authorisation from his fellow-sinners, every Christian man will hold himself obliged, according to the ability which God hath given him, to beseech the unconverted to be reconciled to God.

The religion which Havelock professed assumed that there is no hope of the Divine favour for any man, except through his personal faith in the atoning sacrifice of Christ. Had any stress been laid upon the General's acknowledged moral excellences as the ground on which he might be assured of everlasting life in heaven, he would have cried out, "God forbid." He had done nothing but that which it was his duty to do. Much besides he knew he had left undone. His hope of heaven consequently was what every other man's must be—the hope of a penitent sinner, that the righteousness of Jesus Christ had been reckoned to his account, and that by the power of the Holy Spirit he had been made meet for the inheritance of the saints in light. His good works did not entitle him to salvation: they constituted the proof that he had already obtained it through the exceeding riches of the grace of God. He had been justified by faith—

the only way in which any other man can be justified, seeing that "cursed is every one who continueth not in all things which are written in the book of the law to do them," (Gal. iii. 10.) Havelock, however, took care to shew his faith by his works; patiently continuing in well-doing unto the last; bringing forth fruit unto holiness, the end of which was everlasting life; faithful, and faithful unto his death. Let that death at the Dilkoosha be pondered as it deserves in its most instructive relations to the preceding life:—"Come and see how a Christian can die. I have so ruled my life for more than forty years that when it came I might face death without fear. I die happy and contented. Thank God for my hope in the Saviour! We shall meet in heaven."

Who departs hence like that? Who are tranquil, not terrified; confident, not doubtful; expectant, not desolate; joyous, not sad? The men who rule their lives as did Havelock; the men who live the life which they live in the flesh, a life of faith upon the Son of God; the men who continue and end as they began, rejoicing in Christ Jesus and having no confidence in the flesh.

The place that knew him knoweth him no more. The British Empire mourns his death; the lowering of their colours halfmast-high by one fleet after another as his death was heard of in the United States, told how other nations sympathise with our severe loss. The country expects his memory to be honoured. India demands the celebration of his deeds. The world waits to look in admiration on the monument which we rear to his renown.

Be it so. "The finest site in Europe," the most imperishable material, the noblest effort of our loftiest art, by all means. But one thing first of all. Let every reader of this sketch be personally a follower of him, as he followed Christ. Let him go and imitate his example; and whether he be the statesman, or the magistrate, or the lawyer, or the physician, or the soldier, or the sailor, or the merchant, or the yeoman, or the artisan, or the shopkeeper, or the assistant, or the domestic servant, let him bring out in the habitudes of a religious life henceforward the legible and indelible eulogium,

"SACRED TO THE MEMORY OF
HENRY HAVELOCK, OF LUCKNOW."

THE END.